TOKYO

Quantum 4, Inc.
Per Aspera ad Astra !

Milan   H A N A C E K
Designer of Built Environment

6 4 8 0   Farallon   Way
Oakland
CA 94611.................USA
phone   510 . 404 . 1979
fax   510 . 404 . 1979
quantumfour@usa.com | | |

• • •

Noriyuki Tajima

Tokyo

A guide to recent architecture

● ● ● **ellipsis** K Ö N E M A N N

•••

Tokyo: a guide to recent architecture

CREATED, EDITED AND DESIGNED BY
Ellipsis London Limited
55 Charlotte Road London EC2A 3QT
E MAIL ...@ellipsis.co.uk
WWW http://www.ellipsis.co.uk/ellipsis
PUBLISHED IN THE UK AND AFRICA BY
Ellipsis London Limited
SERIES EDITOR Tom Neville
SERIES DESIGN Jonathan Moberly
EDITOR Vicky Wilson
LAYOUT Pauline Harrison

COPYRIGHT © 1996 Könemann
Verlagsgesellschaft mbH
Bonner Str. 126, D-50968 Köln
PRODUCTION MANAGER Detlev Schaper
PRINTING AND BINDING Sing Cheong
Printing Ltd
Printed in Hong Kong

ISBN 3 89508 286 4 (Könemann)
ISBN 1 899858 01 6 (Ellipsis)

Noriyuki Tajima 1995

Contents

Introduction

The city of Tokyo presents a bewildering array of modern architecture, simultaneously rich, diverse and discordant, which has been built almost entirely within the 20th century. For visitors, Tokyo provides a unique urban experience – a city that is constantly re-forming, adopting new and ever-changing directions. Widely divergent styles and scales exist side by side among a confusing clutter of signs, vending machines and transport systems. In streets with so much to read at times the environment seems indecipherable.

This guide is intended to provide an introduction to the different aspects of Tokyo through a selection of projects that indicates something of the variety of recent architecture rather than a comprehensive catalogue of new schemes. Almost 100 outstanding projects built between 1983 and the present are covered in a collection of the best, the worst and the most stimulating. The selection provides an insight into various social, cultural and economic trends, in addition to the design issues that lie behind the façades. Schemes that are already well known and publicised are included as well as many lesser-known buildings that are symptomatic of specific trends within late-20th-century Tokyo culture.

While most projects are located within the conurbation and city of Tokyo itself, some lie outside, such as Itsuko Hasegawa's Shonandai Culture Centre to the south and Arata Isozaki's Art Tower Mito to the north. The largest project – Kenzo Tange's Tokyo City Hall Complex – covers nearly 400,000 square metres, while the Truss Wall House by Ushida-Findlay Partnership and Atsushi Kitagawara's Higashi-nihonbashi Police Box are a mere 70 and 54 square metres respectively. The range includes the recent spate of massive public schemes – museums, theatres, sports venues and cultural arts facilities – that serve to enhance the capital as well as private residential developments and small-scale interior designs, indicative as they are of the lifestyle and current fashions of the city. Of course, office and commercial developments are most representative of Japan's economic boom of the 1980s and the 'bubble years' that have so dramatically altered the face of its capital.

Two events earlier in the 20th century were also particularly influential in shaping the city and explain the absence of the kind of historical context that exists in most other metropolises. The old Edo-style cityscape was completely destroyed by the Kanto earthquake of 1923, and a modern city plan took shape in the ruins. Then the blanket bombing of World War 2 brought further destruction. Beyond the physical devastation, there was also a profound mental effect. Nationalism was discredited and ties to traditionally held precepts were drastically weakened. For the first time in its long history, Japan was defeated and the people were faced with bankruptcy, both emotional and economic. The post-war period saw the adoption of radical modernisation without reference to past customs and aesthetics, a situation that produced the phenomenon of the 'salary man' – the workaholic who wishes for nothing more than an economically stable life without the weight of a social and cultural heritage. If Tokyo had ever contained the common concept of a city as a kind of moral order, this no longer existed. Instead, it was a developing marketplace whose success depended on the enthusiasm of its participants, willing to embrace new ideas and technology and unfettered by doubts about the evils of progress, looking to the future instead of relying on tradition and the past.

The concentration of political, economic and industrial centres within the greater Tokyo area, due in part to the scarcity of usable land in mountainous Japan, produced a population explosion from 1 million towards the end of the 19th century in an area measuring tens of square kilometres to 30 million inhabitants today in a vast conurbation covering 10,000

Tokyo: a guide to recent architecture

square kilometres. This explosion exactly mirrors the pattern of Japan's rapid economic growth, which finally peaked in the 1980s. Land values rocketed, and property agents, brokers, private companies, banks and the government all combined to accelerate the growth. The situation snowballed until, according to Christopher Wood in *The Bubble Economy*, 'In early 1990, Japan in theory was able to buy the whole of America by selling off metropolitan Tokyo, or all of Canada by hawking the grounds of the Imperial Palace.' This had an enormous impact on architecture. Compared to land, buildings were disposable objects of consumption or advertisements for those who had made the investment, easily demolished or replaced, even if brand new, whenever economic advantage dictated.

In this unbridled marketplace, with corporate offices and commercial spaces rapidly rebuilt and replaced, clients demanded post-modern themes. The first such building was Arata Isozaki's groundbreaking Tsukuba Centre Building of 1983. Here the architect aimed to re-draw classical architectural elements and to introduce a new philosophical discourse through the building's symbolism. The trend – involving quotation, simulation, collage or imitations – was billed as freedom of design. Many other practices followed suit as they became caught up in the wave of commercial growth, turning the outward 'superficiality' to their advantage and exaggerating it to the extreme. Tokyo contains numerous ostentatious 'stage-sets', few of which are worth mentioning. The ease of obtaining work unfortunately resulted in little development of ideas within the emerging 1980s' generation of architects, though a few interesting extravagances were produced, including M2 by Kengo Kuma and Aoyama Technical College by Makoto Sei Watanabe.

It was Kenzo Tange who stated, 'There is no exit for post-modernism' – and then went on to build Tokyo City Hall, perhaps the movement's last great edifice. But a few examples are notable for having developed post-modern themes in a distinctly Japanese way. Shin Takamatsu incorporates the potency of traditional Japanese spaces to extraordinary effect in work such as Earth Tecture sub-1. Fumihiko Maki combines innovative use of materials and spatial depth in striking ways in Spiral and the Tokyo Metropolitan Gymnasium. Hiroshi Hara explores figurative themes and issues of communication in Yamato International. More eclectic forms are assembled by Atsushi Kitagawara in his highly individualistic and poetic projects, while Kijo Rokkaku draws on tradition for his Tokyo Budo-kan. Tadao Ando remains in a class of his own, and needs no introduction here.

Many foreign architects have also been invited to stamp their signatures on the city during the past decade. This was a result of the soaring value of the Yen, which made foreign fees affordable, and the necessity to increase the value of the initial investment in the land through architecture exotic enough to ensure a fashionable following in exactly the same way as a new product might be launched. Philippe Starck's Super Dry Hall and Nigel Coates' Wall exemplify this tendency. More weighty projects have also been undertaken, such as Norman Foster's Century Tower and Mario Botta's Watari-um, and the city has undoubtedly benefited from an injection of diversity from foreign stars.

Whatever the intelligence of the design, architecture in Japan is renowned for the consistent high quality of its detailing and precision finishing, a phenomenon that owes much to the position and organisation of contractors. Massive construction companies act as umbrella organisations that farm out work to small teams of specialists in a system based on the former *Gumi* or Guilds. These are consulted at the early stages of any project and across-the-board discussions ensure that teamwork is co-ordinated and budgets and completion dates adhered to. However, the collapse of the economic bubble has brought to light the spectacular scale of the bribery and bid-rigging that had been going on for years within the industry. Alongside the unmasking of corrupt politicians and the subsequent rolling of heads, entire executive boards were wiped out overnight. The impact this will have on construction remains to be seen. The Takenaka Research and Development Institute exemplifies the better points of construction company-led schemes.

Structure in Japanese architecture is almost invariably heftily built of reinforced concrete and rarely worth noting – neither construction companies nor architects have been willing to experiment or to risk having their buildings and reputations flattened by the earthquakes that periodically rock the city. And as Tokyo sits directly on a major fault, an overdue 'Big One' is an ever-present concern.

The fabric of the cityscape and investigations into its meanings provide fertile ground for future directions. At street level, multi-layered compositions of vast signs and flashing neon mask façades and submerge buildings in sensory displays. Vending machines every 30 metres proffer everything from drinks and meals to disposable cameras and sex aids in a relentless consumer barrage that indicates a city constantly on the move and on the spend. These take their place against a background of diverse materials and structures: glazed, concrete and aluminium façades, steel fire-escapes and concrete tower car parks interspersed with traditional wooden houses and temples. A network of highways and train systems transports the vast population, while golfers practise their swing in floodlit steel-framed cages among the rooftops. TAO Architects pick up these juxtapositions in collage designs such as Gill. And Toyo Ito explores the ephemerality of it all through metaphor in work such as the Tower of Winds, where architecture is a 'thin veil' that wraps the body.

In the mid-1990s, after the heat of the economic explosion, the city is cooling down and memories of the headlong rush to develop are fading. But the architecture of that period remains, directly and indirectly transmitting earlier episodes, preoccupations and values. Even the vacant sites and unlet or unfinished structures tell a story.

Tokyo has been transformed during the last decade. The evidence can be clearly read in its architecture, and no doubt the 1990s will also leave their mark. The endless dynamic of the city is revealed as the post-bubble process begins to unfold.

Acknowledgements

Thank you to so many people: to all the architects and designers who generously supplied material, photographs and drawings; to David Clews and Melanie Brunning as the first readers and test pilots and for their lively discussions about Tokyo; to Keith Collie for photography and sound advice; and to Koji Nagasawa, a generous guide, to Yoshiyuki Tajima, Ei'ichi Kawamura and Yutaka Tada of YEP for their patient support, and to Jonathan Moberly and Tom Neville for giving me the great opportunity to participate in this series. And many thanks to Catherine Powell: this book would never have been completed without her enthusiastic help, comments, corrections, proofreading and encouragement. Finally, thanks to my parents who gave birth to me and raised me here in Tokyo. NT October 1994

Using this book

The city has been divided into fourteen sections. Thirteen are loose geographical areas and the other is the Tokyo Metropolitan Expressway. The nearest station and appropriate subway or railway line are listed below each entry; these services are extremely efficient and an integral part of any visit.

Tokyo has three types of railway: Japan Railways or JR, which includes the essential circular Yamanote Line cut through by the Sobu and Chuo Lines; the Metro lines, which are mostly within this circle; and the private lines such as Seibu, Tokyu, Odakyu and Keio. These last cover the suburban areas and their entrances are usually outside main JR stations.

Addresses are included for all buildings unless specifically refused by the clients. An essential tool is the *Tokyo Metropolitan Atlas*, published (in English) by Shobunsha. The map co-ordinates printed after the addresses in this book are taken from this atlas. The address system is in fact very simple: work backwards, finding the district name which has the suffix '-ku' or '-shi' at the end of the address, then using the given co-ordinates on the map, find the local area name (written in bold in the atlas). The first number of the address is the 'Chome' or neighbourhood number – this is in brackets on the map and the area is designated by a dotted line. Inside this look for the next number which is the block number; this is always extremely small. The last number is the building number. Bear in mind when you arrive that these are often in chronological order so hunt around the block. You can find your bearings very simply by checking the lamp posts, which usually have the area name, Chome and block number posted on them.

1 **North-east Tokyo**
2 **East-central Tokyo**
3 **Bay**
4 **Akasaka, Roppongi**
5 **Nishi-azabu**
6 **Aoyama, Sendagaya**
7 **Shibuya**
8 **Shinagawa**
9 **Shinjuku**
10 **North-west Tokyo**
11 **Setagaya**
12 **South Tokyo
   (Yokohama)**
13 **West Tokyo**

Tokyo Metropolitan Expressway

Tokyo Metropolitan Expressway

The Tokyo Metropolitan Expressway is without doubt the most outstanding and important structure in the fabric of the city. Massive concrete and steel beams support a vast network of roadways that weaves its way through the entire capital, its tentacles stretching as far as the outlying districts of Yokohama, Saitama and Chiba. This traffic roller-coaster flies through and over the cityscape, skimming low-lying rooftops, snaking between towering office blocks and diving into underground tunnels. It adds a further dynamic dimension to the hilly Tokyo landscape, drawing attention to the constantly changing levels and differences between areas, whether industrial, residential or commercial. This three-dimensional, sequential space has no comparison worldwide.

The first section, stretching 4.5 kilometres from Takara-cho in Chuo-ku to Kaigan in Minato-ku, was completed in 1962. Today the expressway's 30 sections exceed 220 kilometres in length. The initial aim was to connect the scattered gymnasiums and stadiums built for the 1964 Tokyo Olympics. Then the expressway became valued as a means of resolving the serious traffic congestion in the city's central areas. At a time when there were relatively few cars, the modern, high-speed road network was greatly admired, but today, as traffic grows heavier and dirtier (and tolls increase), there are many complaints. Traffic jams are frequent and the expressway is often sarcastically referred to as the great 'Tokyo Metropolitan Parking Lot'. On the whole, the city's inhabitants are indifferent to the spectacular feat of engineering on their doorstep.

In the past, Tokyo was a city of rivers and canals (the many beautiful waterfronts can be seen in the *Ukiyoe* paintings of Hiroshige and Hokusai). Today, few remain – most were filled in and transformed into wide urban streets or used as convenient ready-made straight channels for the expressway. Many of those waterways which remain are entirely

1962–

overshadowed by the roadway directly overhead, transformed into sad, gloomy wastelands.

The Nihonbashi River is an example. Tokyo's most famous historic bridge, situated at the heart of the city, is dominated by part of an inner circular expressway that runs above the bridge and riverbanks. The view of the river from the bridge has lost its former beauty and the tops of the classical lamps that used to stand proudly can be admired only by a quick glance from a car window rather than from street level. This change of use from waterway to highway reflects a wider picture of the evolution of the modern metropolis to cope with expanded transportation needs.

The scale and monumentality, weight and strength of the expressway – like ancient Roman city walls – easily overwhelms any of the city's buildings, and striking contrasts are formed against its backdrop. The variously arranged supporting columns are gigantic in scale, in parts as high as 40 metres. They are specially designed to withstand earthquakes, with each section of road capable of moving by a maximum of 20 centimetres. At intersections, where three or four expressways are stacked or layered one above the other, fantastically irregular and acrobatic structures have been created, as at Nihonbashi, Roppongi or Shinjuku. At one such junction, at Azabu-juban just in front of Joule-A, a bizarre little park occupies a triangular plot below the intersection; a playground, shrubbery, fountain and canal fight for daylight beneath its legs. The expressways become 'walls', both enclosures and dividers, creating vacant air-pockets within the dense urban landscape. At other times, encounters with other transportation systems – railways, subways, monorails, bullet trains and pedestrian bridges – produce bewilderingly complex junctions.

During the last ten years, construction of the expressway has been accelerated and in many places it has expanded beyond the level of being

1962–

1962–

a necessary nuisance to becoming the dominant feature that lends character to an area. The expressway to Yokohama offers spectacular views of the developing skyline and its hard shoulder is often blocked with sightseers.

A significant recent addition is the crassly named Rainbow Bridge, completed in 1993 (a visitors' centre and footpath make it accessible to the carless). This beautiful structure connects Shibaura to Thirteen Gochi Pier. Two 126-metre towers support 570 metres of suspended double-deck traffic, with the expressway on the upper deck. The bridge provides a spectacular gateway to the city, with views towards the open sea on one side and the dense multi-level topography of the city on the other: an exhilarating descent into the teeming congestion of buildings and people.

Make friends with a car-owner, plan an expensive taxi ride or take the Limousine bus from Narita to Akasaka, Shinjuku and Yokohama, but don't leave Tokyo without a trip on the expressway.

TOTAL LENGTH 229.2 km
(September 1993), and a
further 100 km are nearing
completion
TRANSPORT 1,130,000 cars per day
FEE ¥700

1962–

1962–

North-east Tokyo

Art Tower Mito

Just over an hour by Hitachi Express from JR Ueno Station is the master-piece of the distinguished post-modernist architect Arata Isozaki. Situated in the old part of the city, the Art Tower is the cultural core of Mito and an attraction for visitors from Tokyo and outlying areas.

As Mito is well known for the cultural history of Komon Mito, one of three Tokugawa families of the Edo period, the local government decided to spend 1 per cent of its annual budget on 'high cultural activities'. A venue was needed. Isozaki was invited to join the project at an early stage by the art curator Yusuke Nakahara, and he helped to organise the whole scheme.

The building accommodates four main functions: a gallery of contemporary art, a concert hall, a theatre and the Mito centennial tower. The various parts are connected by a large square which occupies more than half the site. There is also a sophisticated two-storey conference hall and a museum shop, café and restaurant for day-trippers.

Passing under three oaks at the southern side of the site, visitors are suddenly faced with the three glass roofs of the museum space. A pyramid is set symmetrically at the centre. This geometric gallery space is quoted almost exactly from Isozaki's earlier Museum of Contemporary Art in Los Angeles. The façades are set with porcelain tiles to give the plaza the feel of a European townscape. At the north end, a huge stone placed on the central axis of the square is suspended by thin cables. Water spouts against it, a play on 'Mito', which means 'water gate'.

At the north-western corner, sandwiched between the concert hall and the theatre, is an entrance hall which serves as a connecting chamber for the building's functions. This vertical space is equipped with a pipe organ, and also links the plaza to the street.

The circular theatre, designed as a base for the famous Tadashi Suzuki

Arata Isozaki 1990

troupe, is three tiers high. Most of the audience is seated above and around the stage or just in front of it. The scale is intimate and the action on-stage close and vivid. The columned concert hall has a classical flavour, with a vast moveable drum that descends from the ceiling to control the acoustics.

A 100-metre-high tower to the east of the plaza commemorates the centenary of Mito. This Brancusi-like endless column is made of titanium-panelled tetrahedrons; stacked together, their edges create a DNA-like double helix. Take a lift to the top to experience Isozaki's giddiness.

ADDRESS 1–6–8 Goken-cho, Mito-shi, Ibaraki Prefecture
ASSOCIATED ARCHITECTS Seiichi Mikami & Associates
CLIENT City of Mito
STRUCTURAL ENGINEER Kimura Structural Engineers
CONTRACT VALUE ¥10 billion
SIZE 22,400 square metres
JR Mito – Joban Line from Ueno
ACCESS open Tuesday to Sunday

North-east Tokyo

Arata Isozaki 1990

Arata Isozaki 1990

Tokyo Budo-kan

The Japanese word *Unkai-sanjin* means 'sea of clouds, a man in mountains'. It describes the indigenous Japanese landscape and evokes the spiritual attitude behind the martial arts. The sensuous image for the Tokyo Budo-kan – a mecca for traditional martial arts – came from the idea of mountains overlaying one another and shading off into delicate gradations, as in a traditional Japanese drawing.

The Tokyo Budo-kan contains one large gymnasium, two small halls and an archery court. Kijo Rokkaku's concern is with the gap left by the transition from traditional building methods and materials, which had a recognised cultural significance, to the headlong rush in the twentieth century to adopt new materials, technology and ideas. The Tokyo Budo-kan is a perfect vehicle to address this issue. As Rokkaku says: 'It is not easy to construct a place of traditional function without any historical traces. Traditional culture is well disseminated and familiar, but at the same time easily forgotten and difficult to grasp.' Born into a family of traditional painters, Rokkaku's aim was the creation of a form that would reflect the essence of the traditional psyche. But there is no suggestion of imitation here, of wooden forms, for example; the key was to capture the 'quality of depth' and transform it using modern structural materials such as reinforced concrete and steel.

The solution is simple but effective. A diamond figure is defined as the 'essence of *budo*': one should imagine the stance of a martial-arts player, poised and finely balanced, ready for sudden, fast movement and flexible response in a number of directions, a position that is constantly returned to. This is represented by Rokkaku's 'vertically condensed square', its lowest corner the point of autonomous balance, the moment of readiness for movement. And it is a gesture that is repeated again and again, creating the diamond pattern that dominates the building's vast spaces.

Kijo Rokkaku 1989

Kijo Rokkaku 1989

The Tokyo Budo-kan is best viewed from the approach road from the station through the Ayase Park. Gleaming diamond-shaped galvanised panels cover the steel frame of the roofs. The façade looks like a miniature mountainscape and expresses the *budo* characteristic of intensity and strength in a tranquil state. Beautiful colour changes occur: the building appears pale silver in the morning, gradually turning purple by twilight. As the sun sets, its density and weight appear to increase.

ADDRESS 3–20 Ayase, Adachi-ku [4H 45]
STRUCTURAL ENGINEER Hanawa Structural Engineers
CONTRACT VALUE ¥7400 million
SIZE 17,604 square metres
METRO Ayase – Chiyoda Line
ACCESS open

Kijo Rokkaku 1989

Kijo Rokkaku 1989

N C Building

On 12 September 1992, a Reuters broadcast announced that the architect Peter Eisenman had completed a building in Japan; the famous avant-garde theoretician had embodied his idea of 'textual geology in architecture' at a Tokyo site.

The site, surrounded by narrow downtown-type buildings, is now dominated by a structure that plays on two phenomena: the motion of the Pacific tectonic plates, which cause regional earthquakes, and the geography of the cityscape. These concepts were expressed as blueprint diagrams and then mapped on to the three-dimensional building. The result is a structure that appears to be on the point of collapse, frozen at a moment of transition, shifting and sliding as if during an earthquake. It is visually striking and direct, a childlike metaphor.

The client proudly claims that Eisenman has produced a building about the idea of 'could be' rather than 'should be'. The aim is to create a leading image for Nunotani Corporation, a company which imports ideas for themes and settings for the interior designs of commercial developments such as shopping malls, sports facilities and hotels from the American, and more rarely European, mainstream. The corporation also produces a lifestyle magazine promoting these images. The highly academic American architect was therefore an incongrous choice, selected perhaps to continue the theme of 'Best Hits USA'.

The six-storey building stands on weak, waterlogged ground and required 61-metre-deep foundations to protect it from subsidence and the earthquakes it evokes. It cost an incredible ¥2500 million and took one year to design and a further 19 months to construct. Everything (except the lifts and toilets) is distorted and displaced: windows, floors, walls, columns, even ceilings. Each of the 493 windows is of a different size and it took six months to make the frames (usually a two-week

Peter Eisenman 1992

Peter Eisenman 1992

process). But the effect is limited to the building's appearance, and its structure is in fact of a standard type.

The N C Building's 'crooked house' façade gives way to an entrance hall with stairs down to a basement gallery. Everything is distorted, confusing your sense of balance – an effect that culminates in the gallery space, where almost nothing is vertical or horizontal, producing a sensation of sea- (or building-?) sickness.

Towards the end of Eisenman's lecture at the completion ceremony, a resident from a neighbouring building betrayed his feelings of anxiety: 'It seems to be falling down on to my house. Is it really OK?'. Eisenman replied that the N C Building wouldn't fall down before its neighbours.

ADDRESS 1–21–12 Chuo, Edogawa-ku [4D 48]
ASSOCIATED ARCHITECTS Zenitaka Co, design department of Nunotani Company, Ltd
CLIENT Nunotani Company, Ltd
CONTRACT VALUE ¥2500 million
SIZE 4000 square metres
JR Shin-koiwa – Sobu Line
ACCESS Monday to Friday, 9.30–16.00

North-east Tokyo

Peter Eisenman 1992

Tokyo Sea Life Park

'Going to an aquarium is a simulation of scuba diving.' This simple idea produced an effective design for the Tokyo Sea Life Park. As you leave Kasai Rinkai-koen Station, you see a transparent, apparently buoyant, glass dome at the far edge of the park; beyond lies the bay. The dome is supported by a thin white frame and seems to have just landed on top of a cylindrical building. As you approach, the path meanders, ascends and descends before reaching the dramatic 21-metre-high aquarium entrance. The building itself is barely noticeable – half sunken, a low circular wall.

Standing before the dome as you wait to enter, you realise that the ground is in fact the aquarium's roof, but that this roof appears to be part of the ocean, an illusion achieved by erasing the edge of the building. A shallow pool covering three-quarters of the roof continuously overflows; the water is caught by an invisible lower lip, and this watery boundary merges into the ocean view. You are ready to dive in.

Inside the dome, as if standing on water, two escalators lead you down to the aquarium, which is dark with illuminated tanks. The building contains a total of 2000 tons of water. The highlight is an 'aqua-theatre' where thousands of tuna whirl around you. At the end of the trip, you exit the building on a bay-side 'deck' with sails, as though you had returned safely from your dive.

ADDRESS 6 Rinkai-cho, Edogawa-ku [4J 49]
STRUCTURAL ENGINEER Kimura Structural Engineers
SIZE 14,700 square metres
JR Kasai Rinkai-koen Station – Keiyo Line
ACCESS Tuesday to Sunday, 9.30–16.00

North-east Tokyo

Yoshio Taniguchi 1989

Yoshio Taniguchi 1989

Tsukuba Centre Building

Tsukuba Science City was intended by the government to be Japan's 'Silicon Valley', gathering in a single location the various universities and government research facilities scattered around the capital. When Arata Isozaki was asked to come up with a scheme for a civic centre, he explained the potentially negative aspects of this kind of artificial city-planning, and his criticisms made a strong impression on the client. His appointment was therefore a challenge.

Tsukuba Centre Building is situated in the middle of this large new-town development and contains a concert hall, an information centre, a hotel and a shopping mall reached by pedestrian walkways and bridges set above the traffic level. An empty plaza quoted from the Campidoglio in Rome but reversed and sunken draws attention to the vast scale of the newly built city. But the oval plaza does not set out to celebrate; at one side a strange landscape encroaches and erodes, while an extraordinary artificial tree looks down into the void. This is successful according to the architect's intention, but less so for visitors, who would no doubt prefer more familiar-looking arcades.

The building itself is composed of geometric shapes in materials such as granite and artificial stone, silver-coloured tiles, glass blocks and aluminium panels.

The Tsukuba Centre Building was an epoch-making departure for post-modern design. It ignored all the laws of 'pure' modernism and challenged accepted ideas about originality and functionalism. Each part of the building quotes from an historical style and these are juxtaposed in a jarring manner, irritating architectural historians among others. Isozaki called this technique 'schizophrenic mannerism', suggesting that there is no such thing as a single, true way of approaching architecture. This scandalous assemblage provoked an international debate, prompting many

Arata Isozaki 1983

Arata Isozaki 1983

other architects to explore the issues it raises.

Isozaki published drawings of a ruined Tsukuba Centre Building just after it was completed – functions were made to disappear and only the architectural elements remained as ruins –quoting the precedent of 19th-century neo-classicist architect Sir John Soane's drawing of the Bank of England.

North-east Tokyo

ADDRESS 1-chome Azuma, Tsukuba-shi, Ibaraki Prefecture [1D 106]
CLIENT Housing & Urban Development Corporation
STRUCTURAL ENGINEER Kimura Structural Engineers
SIZE 32,900 square metres
JR Tsuchiura – Joban Line from Ueno
ACCESS open

Arata Isozaki 1983

Arata Isozaki 1983

Takenaka Research and Development Institute

The Takenaka Corporation is one of the most successful contractors in Japan, with a reputation for consistent high quality. Not surprisingly, this much is apparent from the sharp edges and finishes of its showpiece design and development facility.

A circular figure, 153 metres in diameter, prepares the way for further images. Geometric shapes are overlayed on the plan, resulting in a topographical composition of disjunctive walls that produce spatial sequences around, between and through buildings. Beautiful glass cubes are intersected by white walls; slits suggest spaces beyond. Because the building is half sunken, you often cannot tell where you are. Chief architect Yoshiaki Akasaka called the site plan 'the fifth façade' because the spatial quality of the building can be grasped only from a bird's-eye view. In this respect, the site plan works like a city map and the image of the whole can be understood only by assembling fragments of experience.

This maze-like white castle offers a lot of suprising spatial qualities for the 300 people who work here. Marvellous harmonies are generated by the circular walls and traces. Transparent and white planes absorb and transmute the falling light.

The Takenaka Research and Development Institute shows the influence of Eisenman's earlier work, but is better – if not in cleverness, then certainly in quality.

ADDRESS 1–5 Ohtsuka Inzai-machi, Inba-gun, Chiba Prefecture [5E 106]
SIZE 37,715 square metres
METRO Toei Asakusa Line – Keisei Line – Hokuso Kodan Line, Chiba New Town Station
ACCESS none

North-east Tokyo

Takenaka Corporation 1993

Takenaka Corporation 1993

Lala Port Ski Dome, 'Ssaws'

Although at first sight one could never imagine what this vast structure might be, it is, of course, Tokyo's artificial ski slope, built on reclaimed land in the Bay. Standing 80 metres high at one end, 100 metres wide and almost half a kilometre long, it reduces all the surrounding buildings – apartments, factories and warehouses – to a Lilliput.

The ski slope is entirely enclosed with a mountainside of 560,000 square metres maintained at minus 5 degrees. The slope is supported by bridge-like steel frames painted in primary colours and the space below provides hundreds of parking spaces.

The interior perspective is spectacular: to the left a 15-degree incline slope for middle-ability skiers with a 20-degree slope to the right for advanced levels. People at the base are mere specks.

ADDRESS 2–3–1 Hama-cho, Funabashi-shi, Chiba Prefecture [6C 106]
CONTRACTORS Kajima Corporation and NKK
SIZE 109,400 square metres
JR Minami-funabashi – Keiyo Line
ACCESS weekdays 10.00–19.30, weekends 9.00–19.30

Kajima Design 1993

Kajima Design 1993

East-central Tokyo

Wacoal Kojimachi Building

Wacoal manufactures women's underwear and owns Spiral, one of Tokyo's major contemporary art galleries (see page 140). This building is set on a long, narrow site (62 metres by 19 metres) in a prime location. The short façade looks towards the Imperial Palace, creating a meeting of two very different images of prestige: on the one hand, a gleaming corporate headquarters, and on the other the Imperial Palace itself, so powerful it has to be hidden from view behind a low, dense line of trees.

Kisho Kurokawa was well known as a Metabolist in the late 1960s; his current work combines the modern and the traditional, east and west, in a narrative symbiosis. The entrance porch of the Wacoal Kójimachi Building is styled as a landing flying saucer, while inside the ceiling and floor of the entrance hall are decorated with a geometric figure that describes the compass points of a map. Two windows on the eastern façade contain a tracery framework of a celestial map taken from an early 19th-century book. These windows are linked externally into a piston form. The lower floors, housing storage and offices, are angled out and supported by buttresses, and the top-floor Royal Reception Room has a barrel-vaulted roof. This 1930s' Futurist engine is clad in alternate strips of glossy white panels and matt aluminium, primed and ready to steam into the 21st century.

ADDRESS 1–1–2 Kojimachi, Chiyoda-ku [4C 4]
CONTRACTOR joint venture of Takenaka Corporation and Tokyu Construction
CLIENT Wacoal Company, Ltd
SIZE 8300 square metres
METRO Hanzomon – Hanzomon Line
ACCESS none

Kisho Kurokawa 1984

Ochanomizu Square Building

South of Ochanomizu Station is a district of publishers, bookshops and universities, among which lies Arata Isozaki's redevelopment of the head-quarters of publishers Shufu-no-tomo. The original four-storey building was designed in a typical turn-of-the-century neo-classical style by William Merrell Vories, who came to Japan as a missionary in 1904.

Isozaki wanted to retain the original façade as the base for the new enlarged building, which was to contain more offices, a concert hall, a memorial hall at the top and a multi-purpose entrance hall in the middle. But the original structure proved too weak, so the building was entirely reconstructed in terracotta and glassfibre-reinforced concrete panels and Indian beige sandstone to match the old.

Above this replica emerges an ultra-modern towerblock covered with silvery brown-coloured lustre tiles that reflect and subdue the blues of the sky. The new structure is composed of two parts: a five-storey cube faced with rows of wide-framed windows and a modern Italianate balcony on the top. The tower is suspended over the empty courtyard at the core of the building. The two very different styles of this well-matched combination of new and old are brought together at the entrance.

ADDRESS 1–6 Kanda-surugadai, Chiyoda-ku [2G 5]
STRUCTURAL ENGINEER Kimura Structural Engineers
CONTRACTOR Obayashi Corporation
CLIENT Shufu-no-tomo Publishing Company, Ltd
SIZE 22,230 square metres
JR Ochanomizu – Chuo, Sobu Line
METRO Shin-ochanomizu – Chiyoda Line, Ochanomizu – Marunouchi Line
ACCESS public spaces are open

Arata Isozaki 1987

Koizumi Lighting Theatre/IZM

This showroom for a lighting systems company was Peter Eisenman's first project in Japan and a collaboration with a Tokyo-based architect. Kojiro Kitayama is responsible for the bulk of the building, a sharp, plain box which acts as a 'mothership' for the landing of two distorted Eisenman cubes. One is situated at the north-west corner from the first to the third floors and the other at the south-east corner from the fifth to the seventh floors.

The contrasts between the two designers' spaces are more interesting than either on its own: Kitayama and Eisenman, east and west, simple and complex, right-angled and wrong-angled, straightforward and indecipherable. Immediately inside the entrance is a four-storey atrium cut across by steel-railed balconies; the base of one of the inserted cubes can be seen on the ceiling. Its sudden appearance is dramatic, a parasite in a universal-type space. Colourful pink and green walls are layered and fragmented, continuing through the various floors and ceilings and demarcating the cube both inside and outside the building. The entirety can be constructed only in imagination or from the architects' drawings.

ADDRESS 3–12 Kanda-sakuma-cho, Chiyoda-ku [21 5]
STRUCTURAL ENGINEER Ascoral Engineering Associates
CONTRACTOR Taisei Corporation
CLIENT Koizumi Sangyo Company
SIZE 4300 square metres
JR Akihabara – Yamanote, Chuo, Sobu Line
METRO Akihabara – Hibiya Line
ACCESS open 10.00–18.00

East-central Tokyo

Kojiro Kitayama, K Architects and Peter Eisenman 1990

Kojiro Kitayama, K Architects and Peter Eisenman 1990

Metrotour/Edoken Office Building

Atsushi Kitagawara is famous for his poetic and sculptural buildings throughout Tokyo. In the Metrotour/Edoken Office Building, one corner of the elevation rises to a sharp point, creating a wedge shape for the upper storeys. The Belgian glass curtain walls have an almost imperceptible vertical wave and the top of the building seems to lean slightly over the street. At the uppermost point is a meditation room reached by an improbable glass-and-steel-truss exterior staircase. Against the mass of the dark-coloured glass, 25 metallic catwalks jut out, apparently for window maintenance. Seen from street level, the surface of the building looks like an intricate metal web, described by the architect as the 'wings of a dragonfly growing on a glass stalk'. Why, asks Kitagawara, did Brancusi, who dedicated his life to flight, choose the simple bird over an insect?

The metaphor of flight continues in the entrance lobby, where it appears that the wings are beating air. An undulation of draped cloth frozen in cast aluminium forms a reception table and the backrest of a sofa (similar to Kitagawara's earlier project, Rise in Shibuya). A sculpture, made up of a fretwork of metal rods, stands on the black granite floor. The walls are semi -opaque glass and a screen made of strips of metal and mirrors stands to one side.

ADDRESS 1–1–1 Kanda-awaji-cho, Chiyoda-ku [2G 5]
STRUCTURAL ENGINEER Murakami Structural Design
CONTRACTOR Tekken Construction Company, Ltd
SIZE 1870 square metres
METRO Awaji-cho – Marunouchi Line, Ogawa-cho – Toei Shinjuku Line
ACCESS open

Atsushi Kitagawara and ILCD 1989

Atsushi Kitagawara and ILCD 1989

Mitsui Marine and Fire Insurance Company Head Office

This tall block rises from an abundance of dark green foliage which provides a perfect foil for its striking form and colour. The corners of the building are cut back, projecting the façade forward. This is dominated by strips of tinted recessed windows. Sunlight inscribes deep shadows on the niches of the soft grey-brown Canadian granite that covers the exterior. The main structure and services are set at the sides of the building, and at the base a three-storey gap leads to an oval courtyard surrounded by two storeys of offices.

Here the stunning rounded red sculptures of Kyujiro Kiyomizu, visible through the gap, contrast with the rectilinear building. The scale, colour and volume of the objects change our perception of the block, which serves modestly as an immense showcase. The simplicity and harmony of the courtyard are prized qualities of a traditional Zen garden.

ADDRESS 3–9 Kanda-surugadai, Chiyoda-ku [2G 5]
CONTRACTOR joint venture of Kajima, Mitsui, Taisei, Obayashi, Fujita and Zenidaka
SIZE 75,600 square metres
JR Ochanomizu – Chuo, Sobu Line
METRO Shin-ochanomizu – Chiyoda Line, Ochanomizu – Marunouchi Line
ACCESS none

Nikken Sekkei, Ltd 1984

Nikken Sekkei, Ltd 1984

Tokyo International Forum

The Tokyo International Forum was the subject of the first international competition in Japan to be recognised officially by the Union Internationale des Architectes. The brief was for extensive cultural facilities appropriate to a capital city, with 144,000 square metres of space for theatres, museums and arts-related spaces and a contract value of ¥96 billion. Over 2000 people registered for the competition and 395 entries from 50 countries were received. The judging panel included Kenzo Tange, Fumihiko Maki and I M Pei. In December 1989 the first prize and 16 runners-up were announced.

The winner was a New York-based, Uruguayan-born architect, Rafael Vinõly, who narrowly pushed aside British RIBA Gold Medallist James Stirling. Vinõly's scheme provided a smart and cohesive solution to the complex demands of function and circulation while taking into account the surrounding context.

Otemachi and Marunouchi are Japan's economic centres, packed with neutral modern office blocks. A wide band of railways that serve the area passes the eastern end of the site. Two different volumes are presented in the design: regular square blocks that echo the characteristic Marunouchi buildings and a leaf-shaped glass hall that follows the inward-curving line of the railways.

This vast hall, 57.5 metres high, 30 metres wide and 210 metres long, is a spectacular feat of engineering. Supported at either end by an elegant column that swells towards its centre is a roof-level network of tension and co-tension bars that expresses the complex structural forces at play. The frames are as thin and light as possible to create more transparency and are reinforced by cable-structured mullions.

There are many levels of pedestrian circulation. A central path runs north-south between the hall and the main buildings and connects Tokyo

Rafael Vinõly Architects KK 1996

Rafael Vinõly Architects KK 1996

Station and Yurakucho Station and bridges link the upper part of the blocks cross the glass lobby and central path. Flights of escalators lead from the basement to the main buildings, which will eventually include two large theatres. This spectacular project, due to be completed at the end of March 1996, is keenly awaited by Tokyo's citizens

The Tokyo International Forum site was formerly occupied by central government offices, which were moved to Shinjuku to ease traffic and population congestion. The government office building was designed by Kenzo Tange and its removal caused much controversy, since the pure early modernist design was widely admired. It is said that Vinōly received a scandalous ¥7.5 billion on contract for his design – about four times Tange's fee for the new civic centre in Shinjuku.

ADDRESS 3–5–1 Marunouchi, Chiyoda-ku [3G 5]
STRUCTURAL ENGINEER Umezawa, Hanawa, Sasaki and Yokoyama Engineers
CLIENT Tokyo Metropolitan Government
SIZE 144,000 square metres
JR Yuraku-cho – Yamanote Line
ACCESS under construction

Rafael Vinōly Architects KK 1996

Rafael Vinōly Architects KK 1996

DN Tower 21 (Daiichi-Nochu Building)

This is a conservation and redevelopment project for two listed buildings designed by Hitoshi Watanabe. The Nochu Yurakucho Building (1933), on the south-eastern corner of the block, is neo-classical with Ionic columns; the Daiichi Seimei-kan (1938), which occupies the remainder of the site, has a simpler façade of classical proportions seemingly influenced by German Expressionism. After World War 2 both buildings were requisitioned by the Allies and for five and a half years General McArthur's office was on the sixth floor of the Daiichi building.

Shimizu, the original contractor, headed the programme of maintaining the buildings' historical qualities while providing a new high-rise development. Pritzker-Prize-winning American architect Kevin Roche was invited to collaborate.

The western half of the Daiichi was restored to its original condition, but of the rest only the northern façade remains. The Nochu Yurakucho Building was demolished and its Ionic-columned façade rebuilt and extended across the entire eastern length of the block. Into this three-sided shell was inserted a 21-floor high-rise block clad in granite panels – a design that imitates the Daiichi but stretched vertically.

The result, a restrained assemblage of new and old, is elegantly reflected in the nearby Imperial moat.

ADDRESS 1–13 Yuraku-cho, Chiyoda-ku [5F 5]
CONTRACTOR Shilmizu Corporation
CLIENT Dai-ichi Mutual Life Insurance Company and Norinchukin Bank
SIZE 97,900 square metres
JR Yurakucho – Yamanote Line
METRO Hibiya – Chiyoda, Hibiya and Mita Line
ACCESS none

East-central Tokyo

Kevin Roche John Dinkeloo and Associates

War-Dead Memorial Park of Tokyo

This memorial, which replaces a nondescript monument built in the 1960s, commemorates the 160,000 people of Tokyo who died in World War 2. It is conceived as a park for peace: a linear space of calm perpetuity.

The rectangular site is divided into two areas. The street-side section at the north includes a building with facilities for visitors, meeting rooms and space for displays of war history and articles left by those who died, together with a central forecourt. At the southern end is an open square courtyard for ceremonies and worship.

Concrete walls, intermittently cut and fragmented, standing like blank stelae, continue from the main building across the forecourt. In the open remembrance court in front is a further series of fractured walls, set at a shifted angle to the square plan, which appears as a sequence of gates. The effect is formal and directional: as you walk south from the building, the walls guide you, while walking east-west, you cross the gates and boundary lines. This is sequentially effective, but there are no surprises, no sense of the sacred. The effect is also rather lightweight when set against Russian physicist Ilya Prigogine's theory of 'fluctuation', to which the architect intended to refer.

ADDRESS 1–14–4 Kasuga, Bunkyo-ku [5F 13]
STRUCTURAL ENGINEER Gengo Matsui and O.R.S. Office
CLIENT Tokyo Metropolitan Government
CONTRACTOR Kumagai-gumi Company, Ltd, Daikyu-Komuten Company, Ltd
SIZE 925 square metres
METRO Korakuen–Marunouchi Line
ACCESS open

Takefumi Aida Architect and Associates 1988

Takefumi Aida Architect and Associates 1988

Century Tower

The Hongkong & Shanghai Bank building in Hong Kong, with its exposed structure and glass curtain walls, was an international architectural sensation. The client for Century Tower wanted something similar, and this can be seen as a scaled-down version.

The building was Foster's first project in Japan, and it involved a high level of collaboration with local companies. The brief was for an 'intelligent office building' that could accommodate all the functions and services required by a computerised building in the foreseeable future. It was also to include cultural and recreational facilities such as a museum (for the client's art collection), a restaurant and a members' club to make it 'a better place to work' and to extend the building's function beyond office hours.

The design process resembled that of an industrial product rather than architecture, which is often more a case of choosing products. Prototypes and full-scale mock-ups were made for almost every part, all individually designed, tested, pre-fabricated and assembled on site. As a result, many aspects of the building are innovative: for instance, the air-handling units, the lighting/air-conditioning strips and the flooring panels.

The basic plan and design are very simple. Nineteen-storey twin towers are separated by a central, almost full-height atrium which lets natural light flood in. Conspicuous two-storey bracing frames on the south and north façades and within the atrium are structurally autonomous. Each floor is double height with suspended mezzanine floors to create spatial excitement. The service cores are set to either side, freeing the floor space. The west elevation is animated by the movement of the glass lifts, which are visible through the glazed walls, while the glazed east elevation reveals functional details such as stairways, louvered air-handling units and service riser shafts.

East-central Tokyo

Sir Norman Foster & Partners 1991

The interior design is equally simple. Soffit services on the ceiling contain lighting, air conditioning, sprinklers, thermal alarms, emergency lights and speakers within 20-centimetre strips. The rest of the ceiling is covered in white perforated modular steel panels developed to provide maximum reflected light and sound absorbency for the open-plan floors. The lateral service walls are finished in grey metal panels with white panel infils signalling pantries, escape doors, and so on. The flooring panels are dye-cast aluminium raised 15 centimetres to create space for cabling. These panels are unusually large and were subjected to load-bearing tests.

The dominant external feature is the bracing frames. These appear rather heavy due to Japanese fire and earthquake regulations and Foster's usual structural and acrobatic tension is missing.

ADDRESS 2–2–9 Hongo, Bunkyo-ku [6H 13]
STRUCTURAL ENGINEERS Ove Arup & Partners / Obayashi Corporation
CLIENT Century Tower Corporation
CONTRACTOR Obayashi Corporation
SIZE 26,500 square metres
JR Ochanomizu–Chuo, Sobu Line
METRO Shin-ochanomizu–Chiyoda Line, Ochanomizu–Marunouchi Line
ACCESS ground-floor public lobby, Daisen Tea House, Cusit Thien Doung Restaurant and Century Foundation Museum are open

East-central Tokyo

Sir Norman Foster & Partners 1991

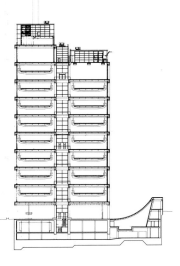

Sir Norman Foster & Partners 1991

Super Dry Hall

Asakusa is where you can still breathe in the atmosphere of *Tokyo Story* together with the incense from the nearby Senso-ji Temple. And today, standing beside the banks of the Sumida River and the Tokyo Metropolitan Expressway, is the spectacular and mysterious object created for the giant brewing company Asahi by French designer Philippe Starck, next door to their new 100-metre-high headquarters building with its golden, beer-coloured glazing.

Asahi first started brewing on this site 100 years ago and the old Asahi Beer Hall was a popular landmark of the downtown area. Its replacement, called Super Dry Hall after the company's most popular brew, or Flamme d'Or after the object winging on top of the building, is said to represent both the 'burning heart of Asahi beer' and a frothy head. It was erected to reflect the social and economic trends of the 1980s, including, of course, the increased consumption of beer. An enormous floating object on a black gravestone-like base, its overstated sense of scale goes far beyond that of the furniture Starck usually designs.

Before beginning this building, Starck had already completed the interiors of a bar and restaurant in central Tokyo, so his work was not unknown to the directors of Asahi Beer. He was introduced by fashion designer Junko Koshino, and the directors decided to take the risk of commissioning him for the new beer hall.

The 360-tonne golden flame was made by shipbuilders using submarine-construction techniques. It is completely empty. Starck describes its importance in terms of 'scale' or 'missing scale', and the sculpture is almost identical to one of his doorhandle designs, intentionally overblown. The four-storey black granite building below the flame widens at the top in an elegant and subtle curve and stands on glass-block steps. Illuminated at night, the base seems to float. Because of its outward lean,

Philippe Starck 1989

Philippe Starck 1989

the closer you get, the bigger it looms.

The entrance is marked by a golden, cloth-like undulating panel and the interior is packed with Starck's surrealistic wit. A two-storey hall contains fat green columns and white marble is used throughout. Padded velvet covers the walls. At one point this is 'folded back' and 'held' by a giant silken thread and tassle to reveal a room behind. The men's urinals have to be experienced!

When it was completed in 1989, many of the old beer-hall regulars complained bitterly about this trendy piece of sensationalism and longed for the cheap accessibility and clumsy cohesion of the original. But after five years, the downtowners seem to have digested the French *esprit*.

This could only have been built in Tokyo.

ADDRESS 1–25 Azumabashi, Sumida-ku [5G 17]
ASSOCIATED ARCHITECTS Makoto Nozawa and GETT
CLIENT Asahi Breweries, Ltd
SIZE 5093 square metres
METRO Asakusa – Ginza Line
ACCESS open

Philippe Starck 1989

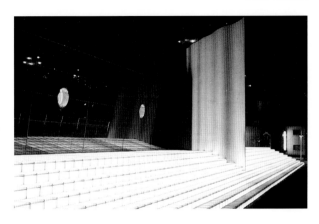

Philippe Starck 1989

Edo-Tokyo Museum

Edo was the name for Tokyo during a 260-year period of strict feudalism and national isolation under the Tokugama Shoganate. It was a time of peace, stability and cultural and economic growth that ended with the arrival of the 'Black Ships' and the Meiji Restoration in 1867, when the city was named Tokyo and began its transformation into a modern, industrialised capital. The museum charts the history of the Edo period, during which time the foundations of the modern city were laid.

After 12 years of planning and development, and ¥59 billion of investment, the museum was finally completed on 28 May 1992. The first and lasting impression is of a crouching, malevolent 'star wars' beast that dwarfs the surrounding buildings, including the beautiful copper roof of the nearby Sumo stadium.

The building is made up of three parts. The two-storey base block houses an entrance hall, a theatre and offices. Above this is an open rooftop plaza on which stand four bulky legs – super columns containing service lifts and so on. These support a further three floors of storage, the 9000-square-metre by 27-metre-high main exhibition space, and a restaurant and café at the top.

The total height, 62 metres, is the same as the Edo Castle which once stood at the centre of the Imperial Palace grounds. To achieve this height, the architect elevated the main space into what would have traditionally been the roof, demoting the middle section to a supporting role, a void. Two long beams (142 metres) span the super columns north and south with a 42-metre cantilever at each end. The façades of the longer sides mirror the main stucture and are a clumsy reference to a traditional Japanese roof.

The building is clad in glaring white fluorine-resin-coated fibre-reinforced concrete panels. As you stand on the steps of the plaza, you become

Kiyonori Kikutake 1992

Kiyonori Kikutake 1992

aware of the vast scale. An escalator travels from the plaza to the underside of the 'belly', enclosed in shiny post-box red panels.

Whether this architecture represents something about modern Tokyo or old Edo is an open question.

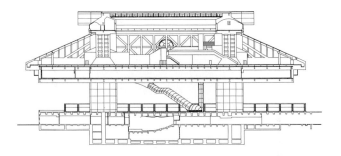

ADDRESS 1–4–1 Yokoami, Sumida-ku [61 17]
STRUCTURAL ENGINEERS Gengo Matsui and O.R.S. Office
CLIENT Tokyo Metropolitan Government
CONTRACT VALUE ¥38 billion
SIZE 48,000 square metres
JR Ryogoku – Sobu Line
ACCESS open

East-central Tokyo

Kiyonori Kikutake 1992

Higashi-nihonbashi Police Box

The traffic island at this junction of three streets is just large enough to house a tiny police box. The project is one of the initiatives of the Metropolitan Police Office, which is concerned to present a more cultural and friendly face to the citizens of Tokyo. The result is a series of lively designs and small-scale post-modern follies by up-and-coming architects scattered across the city.

The role of the neighbourhood police box is described by the architect as 'like an eye in the midst of the city continually recording data.' Thus Kitagawara's design draws on the idea of a 'continuous protective gaze', implying there is an invisible world behind the eye, the backing and authority of the state.

On one side of the building, steel-expanded metal cylinders are piled up to shelter an ovoid inner room of translucent glass which contains a spiral staircase. The other half of the building is very different: a red curved wall and a blue-painted steel frame with a glass and yellow cement wall are inserted into a severe concrete structural frame.

ADDRESS 2–1 Nihonbashi-bakuro-cho, Chuo-ku [2A 6]
STRUCTURAL ENGINEER Ikeda Structure Design Office
CONTRACTOR Toda Construction
SIZE 55 square metres
JR Bakuro-cho – Sobu Line
METRO Bakuro-yokoyama – Toei Shinjuku Line
ACCESS open

Atsushi Kitagawara and ILCD 1992

Lamp posts in Ginza

Ginza is Tokyo's most exclusive shopping, dining and drinking area. Tall buildings (roughly ten storeys) line long, wide avenues and in the evening a spectacular visual feast of vertical neon signs adorns the façades like banners in a traditional woodblock print. Items bought from the expensive department stores are exquisitely wrapped, and in the streets white-gloved chauffeurs in black limousines await their bosses who are spending small fortunes in the many backstreet bars.

A stretch of Harumi-dori Street, which runs from JR Yurakucho Station to Tsukiji, has been upgraded with smart, newly designed traffic signs and streetlamps. The lamps are 10 metres high and made from four poles held together by rings at regular intervals down their lengths. On top is a long cylinder of translucent glass containing a lamp. The bulbs project downwards to produce a soft and calming light. The effect is reminiscent of traditional Japanese lanterns combined with a modern sophistication in keeping with the tone of the area. A further four lamp posts, 15 metres high, stand sentinal at each of the corners of the crossroads in front of the Sony building.

ADDRESS Harumi-dori Street, Ginza Chuo-ku [5E 6]
CLIENT Tokyo Metropolitan Government
SIZE 31 posts along 320 metres
JR Yurakucho – Yamanote Line
METRO Ginza – Hibiya Line, Ginza Line, Marunouchi Line
ACCESS open

GK Sekkei Incorporated 1990

East-central Tokyo

GK Sekkei Incorporated 1990

Bay Area

Egg of Winds

Toyo Ito's UFO-like object forms a symbolic main gate to the largely face-less Ohkawabata River City 21 (see page 88). It was designed as a development of his radical experimental project Pao, a frame just large enough to live in wrapped by a thin membrane and containing demountable furniture suitable to the meet the needs of a modern single woman – a tent-cum-spaceship floating in theskies above Tokyo. The Egg of Winds was also intended to be a 'floating' dwelling unit surrounded by solid residential buildings. But its sheltering function was abandoned and it became more of a comment on the ephemeral nature of the city and the lifestyles of its inhabitants.

In a city where many homes function simply as bedrooms or hotels, Ito observes: 'The residents of Tokyo can, I believe, be compared to nomads wandering in artificial forests. In housing complexes, no one stays at home during the day; even housewives go out. Most of the husbands only come home to sleep … Today in Tokyo buildings are constructed and demolished at a bewildering speed. It is really stunning. Buildings invade the city and gain popularity, then, just as quickly, they are used up and discarded like a piece of paper… Our ideas on semiology and superficiality are developing rapidly, but, even more rapidly, urban spaces have been metamorphosed into symbols and have become superficial.' (*Toyo Ito*, ed. S Roulet and S Soulie, Editions du Moniteur, Paris, 1991) The Egg of Winds echoes this theme – architecture not as monumental and authoritative, but as weightless and lacking solidity, a superficial electronic medium or thin packet.

This electronic rugby ball has a radius of 16 metres at its widest point and 8 metres at the ends. It is made up of 188 aluminium panels and a further 60 in perforated aluminium. In the daytime, surrounded by dull concrete buildings, this metallic object remains mute and inexpressive,

Toyo Ito 1991

but in the evening five computer-controlled projectors inside beam images from five media sources – two VTR, two LD players and one TV programme – on to perforated aluminium screens visible on the outside. These electronic devices create a *Blade Runner*-like atmosphere as the modern dwellers return to their high-rise homes.

ADDRESS 2–2 Tsukuda, Chuo-ku [2F.6]
CLIENT Tokyo Metropolitan Housing Supply Corporation
STRUCTURAL ENGINEER K Nakata & Associates
CONTRACTOR Taisei Corporation
SIZE 118.53 square metres
metro Tsukijima Station – Yurakucho Line
ACCESS open

Bay area

Toyo Ito 1991

Toyo Ito 1991

Ohkawabashi River City 21

Ohkawabashi River City 21, situated beside the estuary of the Sumida River, is a regeneration development by Tokyo Metropolitan Housing Supply Corporation intended for downtown residents forced to leave their homes because of the huge increase in property tax that accompanied the dramatic rise in land prices. Two high-rise concrete residential towers and some medium-sized buildings, nine in all on an 18.65-hectare site, sit incongruously next to the small local housing of Tsukuda-jima, an untouched, traditional fisherman's island. The contrast has been focused on by many photographers and journalists as an example of Tokyo as the 'contradictory city'.

A dramatic new bridge makes it possible for the residents of the 1330 flats to walk to work in central Tokyo.1770 more flats are being built at the east side of the site. Pedestrian paths have been set along the Sumida River and a fountain has been built between the high-rises. All flats offer spectacular panoramic views of Tokyo, 'looking down on the neighbours'. 'That is another town and another world,' said a local from Tsukuda-jima.188

ADDRESS 2 Tsukuda, Chuo-ku [2F 6]
CLIENT Tokyo Metropolitan Housing Supply Corporation
SIZE 2500 flats
METRO Tsukijima Station – Yurakucho Line
ACCESS open

Bay area

Okawabata Renewal Conference 1986–

Okawabata Renewal Conference 1986–

Tokyo Harumi Passenger Terminal

To reach Tokyo from the Pacific, one must first pass under the spectacular new white suspension bridge and gateway to the city, the Rainbow Bridge, then cruise along beside the quiet warehouse quays before arriving at Harumi Passenger Terminal and the start of the mega-city.

The Metropolitan Government wanted to make the terminal a welcoming and impressive symbol and to help revive the neglected waterfront. The terminal contains passport control, luggage handling and farewell or greeting spaces for ocean-going travellers as well as public facilities such as a gallery and an events hall.

From a distance, it first appears as a huge white steel frame, a symbolic 'house' which encloses a glass building with two freestanding lift shafts. The lower part of the structure is made up of overscaled post-modern elements such as the long steps and sloping or circular walls. Large deck-like plazas are filled with bold patterns and expressive streetlamps. Inside the roof frame at the top is a red vista point like a mini- ziggurat for viewing the bay scenery.

This 'pop' architecture has been publicised by fashionable magazines as a glamorous 'date-spot'.

ADDRESS 5–7–1 Harumi, Chuo-ku [4J 7]
STRUCTURAL ENGINEER Orimoto Engineers
CONTRACTOR Shimizu, Toa and Nisshin joint venture
CONTRACT VALUE ¥9400 million
SIZE 17,544 square metres
BUS 13 from Toyosu – Yurakucho Line
ACCESS open

Bay area

Minoru Takeyama 1991

Bay area

Minoru Takeyama 1991

Australian Embassy

This site, home of the Australian Embassy for 50 years, was formerly occupied by an English stately-home-style building set within a beautiful Japanese garden designed during the Edo period. But because of the increasing demands of Australian-Japanese relations (Japan is now one of the biggest markets for Australian exports), more space was needed. It was decided to preserve the garden and the house was replaced by a larger, purpose-built embassy.

The design, which aimed to present a new image of Australia, combines modern metallic materials – aluminium panels and galvanised-steel balconies – with traditional European symmetrical planning and sequences. The ultra-modern façades are a marked contrast to the old Japanese garden. Mita Street is known for its large historical houses hidden from view in surrounding estates. This inter-Pacific collaboration, its frontage made up of a long, smart chain of aluminium boxes, changed its aspect. Functions are hidden behind a single, ordered mask that conveys the totality of the embassy.

ADDRESS 2–1–14 Mita, Minato-ku [3E 8]
ASSOCIATED ARCHITECTS Ashihara
International & Associates
STRUCTURAL ENGINEER Ove Arup &
Partners and Orimoto Engineers
CONTRACTOR Takenaka and Hazama
joint venture
SIZE 22,700 square.metres
METRO Mita – Toei Asakusa Line
ACCESS none

Bay area

Denton Corker Marshall Pty Ltd 1990

Bay area

Denton Corker Marshall Pty Ltd 1990

Gill

The site of this building is the corner of a block where the developers had failed to buy up a small corner building. TAO Architects exploited the space to produce a building with an L-shaped ground plan and two very different façades on the different streets.

The north façade has an understated, elegantly undulating wall of sand-blasted glass blocks with a slender stairwell down to the basement yard; the railings which drop from the street level create a gently curved metal screen. In contrast, the west side is visually dynamic. The entrance is a Japanese pastiche: a bridge with 'post-modern' handrails over a small rock-covered basin. Perforated aluminium framing angles slatted over and over form a gleaming mass of edges and create a menacingly sharp corner on one side.

The different materials are beautifully manipulated and assembled. The idea mirrors the Tokyo environment: a chaos of ideas and textures.

ADDRESS 2–10 Hamamatsu-cho,
Minato-ku [2F 9]
STRUCTURAL ENGINEER Ikeda Sekkei, Ltd
CONTRACTOR Takenaka Corporation
SIZE 1530 square metres
JR Hamamatsu-cho – Yamanote Line
ACCESS none

Bay area

TAO Architects 1991

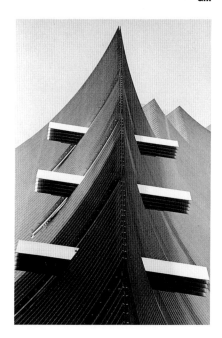

Bay area

TAO Architects 1991

Office of the Japan New Party

Hosokawa was, until recent events, the charismatic modern-style prime minister and his party a fresh force in the moribund Japanese political arena. Although it seems surprising that a political party should invite a relatively unknown modernist designer to style the party office (usually the epitome of conservatism), Howasaka already had a reputation for providing opportunities for such architects as Tadao Ando, Tom Heneghan, Arata Isozaki, Renzo Piano and Riken Yamamoto during his period as governor of Kumamoto Prefecture. And Masaki Morita is from Kumamoto.

This interior is in simple, neat, modern Japanese taste. A meeting room is divided in two by panels of translucent cloth hanging from a walnut frame. The conference table is a large polished slab of wood and the glass-topped coffee table is surrounded by striking black and white leather armchairs. Paper lanterns and an illuminated recessed ceiling panel throw light on this clean, straightforward setting for political discussions.

Bay area

ADDRESS Takanawa, Minato-ku [4G 9]
METRO Sengakuji – Toei Asakusa Line
ACCESS none

Masaki Morita – Design M 1992

Bay area

Masaki Morita – Design M 1992

Akasaka, Roppongi

Kajima KI Building

In a landscaped area behind Akasaka high street is the 'central intelligence' office building of Kajima Corporation, one of the biggest construction companies in Japan. The building was designed for a staff of more than 1000 white-collar workers and includes the departments of architectural design, engineering and information technology.

A four-storey L-shaped glazed atrium with polished stone flooring is at the building's centre. An internal bridge divides this into two areas: an entrance lobby and a rest area where employees can socialise in the sunny oasis atmosphere with its ponds and tropical palms. Set around the atrium are work spaces, rest areas, libraries and variously sized meeting areas for clients equipped with the latest audio-visual presentation screens.

Pacific Telesis, an American company which specialises in facility planning systems, provided an analysis of human interface with the working environment which ensures that the building and its internal layout encourage efficiency, flow and appropriate hierarchical interaction.

Akasaka, Roppongi

ADDRESS 6–5–30 Akasaka, Minato-ku [3C 8]
CLIENT Kajima Corporation
CONTRACTOR Kajima Corporation
SIZE 29,500 square metres
METRO Akasaka – Chiyoda Line
ACCESS none

Midi Architects and Kajima Design 1989

Akasaka, Roppongi

Shun-ju

The theme of this bar is described as 'a fashion designer wearing casual clothes at home'. The intention was to recreate the atmosphere of homeliness once found in traditional bars combined with contemporary stylishness. Traditional Japanese design elements and rich textures are translated into modern compositions. The long narrow space is in fact only 30 tatami mats in size, but it appears much larger.

Every element of the interior is hand-crafted. A Japanese garden runs alongside a long chestnut counter table with a natural bark edge which gives the space a perspectival depth. The ceiling is covered with bamboo and a further dining room is set behind a black metal screen. Lighting is subdued. Rich, tactile earthenware pottery by Seimei Tsuji provides a simple background for the food.

Another bar, Shunju-Hibiki, 4–7–10 Nishi-azabu at Minato-ku, has the same mellow atmosphere.

ADDRESS Akasaka Iinuma Building, 2–16–19 Akasaka, Minato-ku [3C 8]
MAKERS ceramic wall and pottery: Seimei Tsuji, Mio Kaminari; furniture: Shin'ichiro Tani; woodwork: Haruo Tani, Rishichi Amano; earthen wall: Keisuke Imai; garden: Shigeharu Kanetsuna; ironwork: Tokuzo Sunazuka, Shojiro Saito
CONTRACTOR Build Company
SIZE 131 square metres
METRO Akasaka – Chiyoda Line
ACCESS open 18.00–23.00

Akasaka, Roppongi

Takashi Sugimoto 1990

Takashi Sugimoto 1990

Imanishi Moto-akasaka

Shin Takamatsu believes architecture to be an inventory of excessive manipulations, a series of solutions that are 'all nothing but methods for making masks'.

This glittering mask is set on a narrow street. Only 10 metres wide and seven storeys high, it is visually imbalanced. The concave black granite façade has a rounded protruding glass curtain at its centre. The two forms juxtaposed and enlarged over the entire frontage produce an alteration of scale. Details brought together in 'illicit unions' create striking contrasts: 'the inarticulate articulation of the whole and its parts'. The interior offices, however, are entirely conventional.

Kirin Plaza, a bizarre elongated building with four huge lanterns in flashy downtown Osaka, is by the same architect. Imanishi Moto-akasaka is on a smaller scale and situated in a calmer area, but the impact is just as strong.

ADDRESS 1–1–6 Motoakasaka, Minato-ku [3B 8]
STRUCTURAL ENGINEER Yamamoto-Tachibana Architects & Engineers
CLIENT Imanishi Company
CONTRACTOR Kajima Corporation
SIZE 1470 square metres
METRO Akasaka – Chiyoda Line
ACCESS none

Akasaka, Roppongi

Shin Takamatsu 1990

Swedish Embassy

Embassies were not immune from the effects of the inflation in land prices and the associated property tax. Many had to move into commercial offices, while others added new storeys to existing buildings to raise rent to help pay the land tax. This site was owned by three organisations, including the Swedish Embassy, each too small to develop their building to their best advantage because of legal restrictions. This development was possible only by joining forces so the larger ground area would permit the building to rise to a greater height.

The building slopes from eight storeys at one end to three at the other to accommodate the 'off-site shadow control' limitations. A sweeping curved wall in Swedish red granite contains the complex on the street side. Wooden window frames, greenery and freestanding sculpture give the site a characteristically Swedish sense of naturalness and warmth, a good example of a more friendly aesthetic in contrast to the high-tech materials favoured by many Japanese architects.

ADDRESS 1–10–3 Roppongi, Minato-ku
ASSOCIATED ARCHITECTS Irie Miyake Architects and Engineers
CONTRACTOR Takenaka Corporation
SIZE 10,360 square metres
METRO Kamiyacho – Hibiya Line
ACCESS none

Akasaka, Roppongi

Michael Granit 1991

Michael Granit 1991

Beauty Salon Shima Nogizaka

Hairdressers need to provide their clients with the relaxed atmosphere of a temple dedicated to the 'science of the self' and an ambience that reflects their role as arbiters of the latest trends. This beauty salon is designed by an up-and-coming architect working in the style of Shin Takamatsu and to a lesser extent Tadao Ando, both of whom have set the pace for fashionable commercial interiors.

A jumbo-jet-sized wing on the ceiling, made from curved metal sheets, dominates the white-painted concrete second-floor space. This feature is visible from street level, luring in intrigued punters. Three moveable stands, each with four mirrors and topped by an array of tubular lights on mechanical arms, are positioned around a thick square column. A room for washing hair has mesh screens and metal details. A restricted number of design elements provides an effective contrast to the overscaled wing and the minimalism of the bare floor and walls.

Akasaka, Roppongi

ADDRESS 2F Pacific Nogizaka,
9–6–29 Akasaka, Minato-ku
CLIENT Island Company, Ltd
CONTRACTOR Ishimaru
SIZE 130 square metres
METRO Nogizaka – Chiyoda Line
ACCESS open 10.00–20.00

Yasuo Kondo 1988

Akasaka, Roppongi

Yasuo Kondo 1988

Oxy Nogizaka

A concrete façade with a single window, displaying a modesty more usual in an unobtrusive rear wall, announces the theme of 'absence of noise'. The lack of mediation between inside and outside – a reflection of the discontinuity of the city – could be seen as a contrast with European façades, which function as frames between private and public and whose density provides the street with continuity.

Eight storeys of office space are set behind a curved wall that negotiates the corner of a complicated intersection of streets. The façade acts as a boundary and changes depending on the direction from which you approach. According to the architect, 'It must have scenes where different worlds intersect. The worlds must not be clearly differentiated but be fallen in on each other.' (*Discontinuous City, Kiyoshi Sey Takeyama: Architect*, Rikuyosha Publications.)

Akasaka, Roppongi

ADDRESS 7–2–8 Roppongi, Minato-ku [5C 8]
STRUCTURAL ENGINEER TIS & Partners
CONTRACTOR Asanuma-gumi Construction
SIZE 1000 square metres
METRO Nogizaka – Chiyoda Line
ACCESS none

Kiyoshi Sey Takeyama and Amorphe 1987

Kiyoshi Sey Takeyama and Amorphe 1987

Nishi-azabu

Kon'yo Shen'te

A visitation to Tokyo in September 1986 by Austrian deconstructivists Coop Himmelblau produced a dramatic shop interior. The design period started on 1 September, construction was completed on 18 September, and the architects left as suddenly as they had arrived – without comment. The design was determined by spontaneous modelling rather than by planning. Coop Himmelblau's method involves 'automatism' – translating arbitrarily constructed models into plans and elevations and finally transforming these back into a construction, giving the end result a complex and unintelligible quality, with residual traces of the original activities.

The shop (whose name means 'five senses') is situated in the basement of an ordinary white-tiled apartment block. A 'mantis arm' made from green steel panels and a stainless-steel pipe emerge on the outside, signalling that something unusual is going on below. Inside, this becomes a large, elaborate display case for glass, pottery and other goods. The design spills throughout the space, both incorporating and disregarding existing features such as columns. Glass, steel and wood perform an extraordinary spatial balancing act.

ADDRESS 3–17–15 Nishi-azabu, Minato-ku [4D 8]
CLIENT Jiva Company, Ltd
CONTRACTOR Nakamura Tensetsu
SIZE 96 square metres
METRO Hiroo – Hibiya Line
ACCESS open for shopping (not for examining)

Nishi-azabu

Coop Himmelblau 1986

Coop Himmelblau 1986

Joule-A

This thirteen-storey building by Harvard graduate Edward Suzuki faces a double-deck highway. Seen from a car, the curved façade, about 50 metres long, seems to move along with you and is at its most dynamic as you accelerate away from it.

The most striking feature is a ragged skin of perforated-aluminium panels attached to galvanised truss frames on the upper part of the building. Terraces located immediately behind the framework are filled with bamboo, masking the plain façade which is revealed only occasionally through the gaps. Fully exposed columns and curved beams encircle a three-storey void containing a public plaza at the base of the building. The rear façades, the radii of the quarter-circle plan, are clad with monotonous aluminium panels.

The development dates from the end of the bubble period (the client is a subsidiary of car dealers specialising in Rolls Royce, Aston Martin, and so on). There is a restaurant in the basement and a deluxe sports club and residential space on the upper floors. The client expected high-flying businessmen to live, work, dine and work out within the building, but the bubble burst as it was completed. After being mostly empty, it now houses an American-founded college.

ADDRESS 1–10–1 Azabu-juban, Minato-ku [4E 8]
STRUCTURAL ENGINEER Tanaka Engineers
CLIENT Azabu Building Company, Ltd
CONTRACTOR Kajima Corporation
SIZE 9860 square metres
BUS HASI-86 from Hiroo or Shibuya, TA-70 from Roppongi
ACCESS limited

Edward Suzuki 1990

Nishi-azabu

Edward Suzuki 1990

Azabu Edge

Some 20 years ago work was begun on a tunnel crossing beneath Roppongi Street to connect to Azabu and Aoyama. But the government failed to purchase the land needed to complete the project, so the road looped back up to Roppongi Street, leading nowhere. The tunnel and loop became a much-talked-about absurdity, a graffiti-scrawled dead-end and wasted interstice of the city. At this site, Suzuki explores the edge condition.

The building, containing a bar, shops and offices, is roughly made from unembellished concrete scarred in places by pneumatic drills. A boxed window extends unnecessarily into the outside space and a rusted steel bow column on the façade is too weak to have any structural value. Steps around the building produce maze-like connections and a flight of steps that also functions as a lower roof provides views over the area.

Recently the government completed the road connection. Buildings along the new street are now well ordered and Azabu Edge part of a continuous wall. But Suzuki's landmark still serves as a reminder of a former state and of the transitory nature of the city.

ADDRESS 1–1–1 Nishi-azabu, Minato-ku [4C 8]
STRUCTURAL ENGINEER Yamabe Structural Engineers
CONTRACTOR Takenaka Corporation
SIZE 1300 square metres
METRO Roppongi – Hibiya Line
ACCESS limited

Nishi-azabu

Ryoji Suzuki 1987

Nishi-azabu

The Wall

The cityscape of Tokyo is remarkable for its almost complete absence of built continuity. It has been constantly reconstructed since the great earthquake in 1923 and more recently since World War 2.

Nigel Coates' Wall is set along the main street from cosmopolitan Hiroo to Aoyama and across the street from a Tadao Ando building that once housed a Coates-designed bar. It abruptly introduces history in the form of Ancient Rome. During construction, a vast hoarding declared: 'The concept for the building revolves around a wall of monumental proportions – a wall which could have been built by the Romans, a wall of stone and giant arches, a wall which could have encircled cities. But unlike the ruins of Rome, this wall is both ancient and still being built. Atop its giant cornices, blocks of stone lie waiting to be placed. Sculptures in the form of ancient building cranes suggest that the building is continuing to grow, towards the future into the 21st century.'

Italian bricklayers were flown in to apply the final texture to this artificially ruined wall. A Victorian gasometer-like cast-iron frame in front of the façade supplies a further archaeological layer and inverted aircraft undercarriage wheels, cast in bronze, are used at the cornice. Visitors to the bars within may ascend stairs on the outside so that seen from the street they weave past and present to become 'characters in an architectural drama'.

The prohibitive cost of land in Tokyo necessitates a fast recouping of investment, and a novelty such as this draws in the crowds. Since the British architect designed the Metropole restaurant in 1985 – a combination of 'an English gentleman's club and a European café with traces of decay' – in collaboration with creative 'space producer' Shi Yu Chen, the duo are regarded by many followers as almost mythical talents who can be relied upon to produce imaginative commercial hits, albeit short-

Branson Coates Architecture Ltd 1990

Nishi-azabu

Branson Coates Architecture Ltd 1990

lived ones. Their unbounded imagination and the fluidity of their approach are welcomed by many as breaking away from the idea of the ideal building – whether western or eastern – and as signalling a new kind of hedonism. But today, given the short attention span of the fashion crowd and the post-bubble economic climate, the Wall's appeal is somewhat faded. Male exotic dancers and the occasional Cobra convertible parked outside provide the icing on the cake.

ADDRESS 4–2–4 Nishi-azabu, Minato-ku [5D 8]
ARCHITECTURAL PRODUCER Creative Intelligence Associates Inc.
ASSOCIATED ARCHITECTS Dan Architecture Company, Ltd
STRUCTURAL ENGINEER K3 Institute Company, Ltd
CLIENT JET Planning & Architecture Company, Ltd
CONTRACTOR Fujita Company, Ltd
SIZE 830 square metres
METRO Hiroo – Hibiya Line
ACCESS open

Nishi-azabu

Branson Coates Architecture Ltd 1990

Nishi-azabu

Branson Coates Architecture Ltd 1990

Penrose Institute of Contemporary Arts

Penrose is the name of the founder of the avant-garde Institute of Contemporary Arts (ICA) in London, and this is its sister gallery and Tokyo link-up, as the satellite-dish object at the top of the building suggests. Set at the southern end of Coates' Wall (see page 120), the gallery occupies an 85-square-metre corner site facing south-east. Eight storeys, including three double-height floors, house a total of 340 square metres of exhibition space.

The collaged façade contains contradictory narratives. Four Doric columns at the entrance signify the permanence of European public buildings as well as an association with 'rockets about to be launched'. The exterior is covered in solid terracotta tiles, their heaviness relieved by a network of stud lights. Unfortunately, almost one-third of the tiny floor space is occupied by the stairs and lift; this roomy lift-hall seems to be the poor relation in comparison to the ICA's London facilities.

ADDRESS 4–2–5 Nishi-azabu, Minato-ku [5D 8]
TOTAL PRODUCER Creative Intelligence Associates Inc.
ASSOCIATED ARCHITECT Gomi Architecture
STRUCTURAL ENGINEER T.I.S. & Partners
CLIENT Kaishin Sangyo
CONTRACTOR Maeda Construction
SIZE 340 square metres
METRO Hiroo – Hibiya Line
ACCESS open

Nishi-azabu

Branson Coates Architecture Ltd 1993

Nishi-azabu

Aoyama, Sendagaya

Collezione

Of the several works in Tokyo by the Osaka-based architect Tadao Ando, this is probably the best example to visit. Ando's minimalist use of concrete and the rich qualities of light and shadow is his work have been lauded in architectural schools worldwide. Yet he himself is entirely self-taught, starting his career as a boxer, a sport whose discipline and rigour he has carried over into his architecture.

The concrete building is located in an exclusive fashion street. The neighbouring brick From-1st, also a Hamano Institute directed building, set the stylish tone of the street in 1975. Collezione, located at the end of the street, is its focal point.

Almost half the building is below ground, but it reads as a continous seven-storey structure. The lowest level contains parking for 40 cars. A luxury gymnasium with a 20-metre pool occupies the first and second basement floors below couture fashion shops on the ground and first floors. A showroom and gallery are located on the second and third floors together with the owner's penthouse flat.

The inspiration for this 'strata architecture', as Ando calls it, came from a visit to an Indian well: 'Step by step, down towards the water's edge, passing strata, the eyes perceive gradations of light and the skin experiences a reduction in temperature' (Tadao Ando, translated by the author). According to the architect, the degree of luminosity could be described by a quadratic equation which refers to the behaviour of reflected light in a sharply decreasing curve.

The plan consists of two long rectangles set apart by a 13.5 degree interstice. These are gridded by 6.15-metre-span concrete frames. A 21-metre-diameter cylinder, made of glass and aluminium panels, is inserted into the larger rectangle, projecting on to the street. A cube has been added at the top.

Aoyama, Sendagaya

Tadao Ando 1989

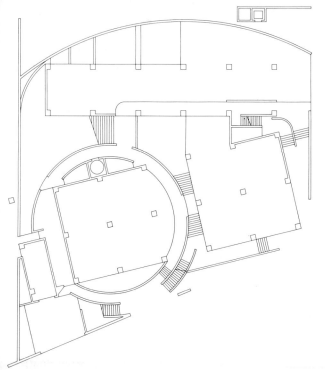

The cylinder is circumnavigated by steps and walkways spiralling upwards and downwards and leading to bridges and platforms that sometimes turn back on themselves, so the visitor is confronted with a view of the journey undertaken so far. Combinations of volumes and voids produce a sequential and spatial dynamism: ascent and descent, soaring ceiling heights and sudden low spaces, areas open to the sky or enclosed. This Esher-like maze turns visitors into both 'viewers' and 'viewed'.

A flight of steps leads directly from street level down to the three-storey void. The climax occurs as you descend the steps from the first basement courtyard to a second, where the space opens out vertically with each step and also widens to follow the curve of the cylinder. A vast facing wall provides a backdrop for Ando's unearthly manipulation of reflected light and an opportunity to experience his 'spiritual space' deep in the strata.

Aoyama, Sendagaya

ADDRESS 6–1–3 Minami-aoyama, Minato-ku [5C 8]
TOTAL PRODUCER Hamano Institute
STRUCTURAL ENGINEER Ascoral Engineering Associates
CONTRACTOR Obayashi Corporation
SIZE 5700 square metres
METRO Omotesando – Chiyoda, Ginza, Hanzomon Line
ACCESS open

Tadao Ando 1989

Aoyama, Sendagaya

Tadao Ando 1989

Ambiente International

Aldo Rossi's architectural drawings have been likened to the fantasy buildings in de Chirico's Surrealist paintings and have had a strong influence on 1980s' post-modernism. For importer of Italian furniture Ambiente International, the classical archetype has been stripped down, maintaining its proportions but without the usual ornamentation, capitals or thickening in the columns, giving the familiar symbolism a lightness and grace.

The area incongruously combines sophisticated fashion and design offices with traditional housing and small family businesses. The scale of Rossi's scheme is far smaller than that of his earlier project in Genoa, but is appropriate to the narrow streets and surrounding buildings. Two-thirds of the 400-square-metre showroom is situated in the basement with the rest on the ground floor. Above are two floors of offices.

The rectangular box measures 25 metres by 9 metres and is situated on a corner. The longer façade is ordered with repeated windows and columns. Steps running along the side of the building lead from the pavement to the basement and there are two octagonal cupolas on the roof. The main entrance is on the shorter eastern façade to give a long processional sequence into the interior. A deep blue marble wall provides an exotic backdrop for an excessively thick triangular white marble pediment supported by two solid columns.

The interior continues similar classical themes. The Italian-proportioned double-height reception room has stuccoed walls. An elegant spiral staircase at its centre with thin steel handrails descends into the basement showroom which includes some examples of the architect's furniture. Above this is a circular light-well running up to one of the cupolas overlooked by a second-floor balcony.

The literal translation of Rossi's two-dimensional drawing into a three-

Aoyama, Sendagaya

Aldo Rossi 1991

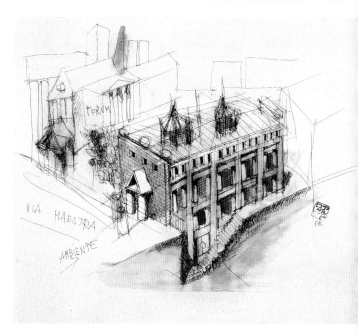

Aldo Rossi 1991

dimensional building is at times unsatisfactory. The deft touch and sensual quality of the original drawing and the interest supplied by the distorted angle of the axonometric view are completely absent. The result is like the memory of a favourite illustration from a book of fairy tales that loses its charm and seems overblown when 'made real' in theatre or film.

Aoyama, Sendagaya

ADDRESS 4–11–1 Minami-aoyama, Minato-ku [5C 8]
ASSOCIATED ARCHITECTS Progetto Cappa/Kitai Architects & Planners Inc.
CLIENT Ambiente International Inc.
CONTRACTOR Obayashi Corporation
SIZE 743 square metres
METRO Omotesando or Gaienmae – Ginza Line
ACCESS to showroom

Aldo Rossi 1991

Aoyama, Sendagaya

Santeloco

The interior of this mirror and glass manufacturer's showroom is more like a museum: plain white walls, lighting rails on the ceiling and a light tan carpet throughout. Set within this space are Kitagawara's extraordinary objects.

A reclining black cone suspended from the ceiling seems to float in the centre of the room, its sharp point only 3 centimetres from the floor: 'an aphorism on the onrush of knowledge'. Beside this is an amorphous piece of mesh hung from cables. A black urethane-coated ovoid table is set beside three chairs with curved aluminium backrests. A distorted set of shelves designed by a computer incorporating a 'fluctual shift' could be a simulated landscape. Each object is autonomous, like exhibits that are part of some mysterious installation.

ADDRESS 1F Aoyama Konparu Building, 3–1–7 Minami-aoyama, Minato-ku [5B 8]
CLIENT Asahi Glass Company
CONTRACTOR Tanseisha Company, Ltd
SIZE 178 square metres
METRO Gaienmae – Ginza Line
ACCESS open

Atsushi Kitagawara + ILCD 1990

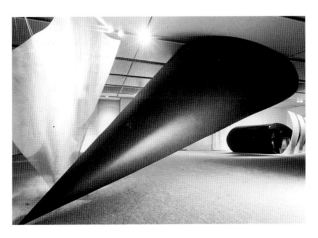

Atsushi Kitagawara + ILCD 1990

Muji, Aoyama 3-chome

Muji, a chain of lifestyle stores offering simple but sophisticated kitchenware, clothing and stationery, is rapidly expanding in London and other cities. Muji literally means 'plain', but the Japanese name 'Mujirushi' translates as 'no-brand'; ironically this supposed anonymity has become a designer label in its own right. Muji was created during the 1980s as an offshoot of the Seiyu department store with Kazumitsu Tanaka as art director. Takashi Sugimoto contributed the interior identity and succeeded in cultivating an atmosphere of anonymity and neutrality by using recycled and 'undesigned' materials.

This Aoyama branch is a good example. Two materials dominate: salvaged wood and steel panels collected from demolished houses and scrap-metal merchants. This new wave of Japanese style takes its inspiration from mass production: the plain living style of old Japanese farmhouses recycled into the modern industrial age.

Aoyama, Sendagaya

ADDRESS 2–12–8 Kita-aoyama, Minato-ku [5B 8]
CLIENT Ryohin Keikaku Company
CONTRACTOR Hakusui-sha
SIZE 495 square metres
METRO Gaienmae – Ginza Line
ACCESS open 10.00–20.00

Takashi Sugimoto and Super Potato 1993

Takashi Sugimoto and Super Potato 1993

Spiral

This building is the result of a philanthropic gesture on the part of the lingerie company Wacoal, which was concerned to contribute to the 'upgrading of daily life' by setting up a cultural 'antenna' that would gather the visual arts, theatre and music under one roof together with a fashionable bar, café and restaurant. Fumihiko Maki resolved a complex programme with a single well-articulated idea – the spiral. This is embodied throughout the building, both inside and out, giving a sense of cultural flow that is both mentally inspiring and physically uplifting.

The entrance hall is set back from the street behind a series of columns. A narrow recessed light placed down the centre of the ceiling sets up perspective lines and depth. Three steps lead up to a carpeted café area bounded by square dark green granite-panelled columns which support a low ceiling. The lighting is shadowy. At the far end of the café is a circular 'stage' on to which light pours down from the semi-circular skylight at the top of the building. A raised level running along the right of the café to the stage provides hanging space for art works.

This gallery 'street' is reached by ascending a flight of eight steps on the right of the entrance hall, revealing a dramatic contrast in height and atmosphere in the form of a well-lit double-height ceiling. Seen from the gallery, the café appears to be situated in a two-storey interior building with windows set in the upper storey. However, visitors relaxing in Hoffmann Fledermaus chairs have the impression of being in a street café from which they can contemplate the art works and their viewers.

The centrepiece of the building is an apparently freestanding spiral ramp with a diameter of 15 metres that runs from the circular stage to the second storey. This is set against a white marble wall dissected by a slanting cleft in its surface. The ramp is separated from the wall by a small gap which allows light to fall unimpeded to the ground floor. Two

Fumihiko Maki & Associates 1985

Aoyama, Sendagaya

Aoyama, Sendagaya

Fumihiko Maki & Associates 1985

supporting beams are cleverly concealed. The main bulk of the spiral is camouflaged with dark red paint, while the thin white outer edge and delicate balustrade reinforce the impression that the structure is floating. A heavenly ascent under the shower of white light from the skylight brings the supplicant only to a second-floor designer merchandise shop.

Passing through the shop, a stepped corridor hanging above Aoyama Street completes the connection back to the spiral, leading down to the entrance hall or up to the foyer of the multi-purpose hall on the third floor. Here a large square opening frames a wire sculpture by Aiko Miyawaki.

The flowing circulation is reflected on the façade, where squares of different materials form a spiralling collage. The sharp etched lines between the aluminium panels, set without the usual sealing compound, accentuate the flatness of the walls. White *shoji* (semi-opaque) glass is set within aluminium frames that draw a sharp grid of shadows. This is contrasted with recessed rectangles of transparent glass walling. To this composition a white cone and curved wall have been added.

Deliberately asymmetrical, submerged among the surrounding façades, Spiral doesn't project any authority, but contributes to the sense of fragmentation in the Tokyo cityscape.

ADDRESS 5–6–23 Minami-aoyama, Minato-ku [5C 8]
STRUCTURAL ENGINEER Toshihiko Kimura Structural Engineers
CONTRACTOR Takenaka Corporation
SIZE 10,560 square metres
METRO Omotesando – Chiyoda, Ginza, Hanzomon Line
ACCESS open

Aoyama, Sendagaya

Fumihiko Maki & Associates 1985

Tepia

The public face of the Machinery and Information Industries Promotion Foundation, the building's optimistic name Tepia is derived from a combination of the words 'technology' and 'utopia'. Just ten minutes walk from Maki's earlier Spiral building (see page 140), Tepia exhibits a similar sharp detailing and strong plan. The building contains exhibition spaces with a sports club in the basement and an exclusive members' club at the top.

The project is a taut composition of walls, floors and roofs. The clean edges of the aluminium panels that make up the façades are intentionally revealed. The sheet glass and a curved wall of glass blocks draw light into the long grey aluminium-panelled entrance lobby.

An exterior flight of steps provides direct access to the second storey. Set within an abstract garden, the simple outward flaring at the stair's base gives it a sculptural quality. A shallow black-and-white-bottomed pool serves as a reflector and at the rear of the garden is a series of stone cubes arranged within a chequered area.

ADDRESS 2–8–44 Kita-aoyama, Minato-ku [5B 8]
STRUCTURAL ENGINEER Toshihiko Kimura Structural Engineers
CONTRACTOR joint venture of Kajima, Shimizu and Hazama
SIZE 13,810 square metres
METRO Gaienmae – Ginza Line
ACCESS open 10.00–18.00

Fumihiko Maki & Associates 1989

Aoyama, Sendagaya

Sendagaya Intes

Originally Takenaka designed and built this eleven-storey building as its own offices. But it was spotted by a managing director of Apple Japan, which was looking for a new, larger space, and Takenaka was persuaded to rent out its stately glass tower. The building stands in an extensive landscaped garden, towering over the low-lying Tokyo Metropolitan Gymnasium (see page 150) and nearby residential buildings. The distinctive sharp detailing is a signature of the contractors.

The outside walls are freed from any structural purpose. The glazing frames – vertical aluminium rods with flat-sectioned cross-pieces – draw thin clean lines over the building. The overall luminosity is further emphasised by the almost semi-circular plan. As you approach, the high-quality transparency of the sheet glass becomes more apparent and Apple computer displays come into view.

ADDRESS 1–14–5 Sendagaya, Shibuya-ku [1F 29]
CLIENT Takenaka Corporation
CONTRACTOR Takenaka Corporation
SIZE 10,602 square metres
JR Sendagaya – Sobu Line
ACCESS none

Takenaka Corporation 1991

National Noh Theatre

Noh is Japan's oldest form of theatre. It began to flourish in the 14th century, though its origins go back much further. It represented high culture for the samurai classes, while kabuki or bunraku provided spectacle for commoners.

This essentially traditional theatre, designed by a master of modern architecture, is intended to promote noh plays as national treasures. Exhibition rooms and educational facilities are provided in addition to the theatre itself. Modern planning has been masked by traditional features in order to cultivate an appropriate sense of tradition.

The exterior is characterised by layers of slightly curved roofs: two main square roofs surrounded by lower ones, all surfaced with aluminium louvres. The interior spaces, placed around an inner court containing greenery, have traditional elements such as columns and wooden details.

Noh theatre takes place on a square, roofed main stage at the centre of the auditorium connected to the backstage area by a long narrow bridge to one side that allows the actors to enter in a drawn-out and formalised manner. A traditional house façade is attached to the opposite wall of the stage. The spectacle consists of lyrical dance-dramas enacted by masked actors to the accompaniment of traditional music. One endeavours to depart as slowly and elegantly.

ADDRESS 4–18–1 Sendagaya, Shibuya-ku [1F 29]
CLIENT Japan Arts Council
CONTRACTORS Hazama Corporation, Sumitomo Construction
SIZE 10,249 square metres
JR Sendagaya – Sobu Line
ACCESS open

Aoyama, Sendagaya

Hiroshi Ohe 1983

Hiroshi Ohe 1983

Tokyo Metropolitan Gymnasium

As you leave Sendagaya Station, a low, spreading metallic building comes into view that uncannily resembles a traditional samurai helmet compressed and transported into the space age. It is part of a gymnasium complex of three buildings: the spectacular main building or arena, a square box containing a swimming pool and a smaller sub-arena with a stepped pyramid roof. These are situated within a square 4.5-hectare site with open space around each. The buildings continue below ground over 4.4 hectares containing further facilities.

The most dynamic element is the stainless-steel roof of the 120-metre-diameter arena. Three different truss arches spanning east-west lie next to each other, producing a mechanical folded effect at either end. Tension rings tighten the joints to cope with the lateral loading, making the roof structurally independent from the walls and columns: 'two leaves lying over each other on four large columns'.

The height of the project was kept to below 30 metres and the combination of the three distinctive rooflines is intended to create a 'multiple landscape' rather than a 'singular union'. The hilltop site overlooks Tokyo Stadium and the Sendagaya Intes building (page 146).

The three volumes are deliberately positioned to refer to the surrounding context. The main arena is set well back to allow its entire width to be viewed from the station. Here at the north-western corner is a complex entrance that includes a fountain. Diagonal lines from this edge lead visitors towards each of the three buildings. The swimming-pool box at the south-western corner mediates between the vast scale of the site and the regular-sized buildings nearby. The pyramid modestly encloses the south-eastern edge of the park and prevents the scale from being overwhelming.

Those familiar with the gymnasium that formerly occupied the site –

Fumihiko Maki & Associates 1990

Aoyama, Sendagaya

Fumihiko Maki & Associates 1990

a series of blocks in a square layout – were taken by suprise by the character of the new site as a 'modern garden'. Each point reveals a completely different scene and the landscape changes as you walk through, a characteristic of the traditional Japanese garden. Thus Maki has managed to avoid the 'big is a bore' syndrome typical of so many large-scale buildings.

ADDRESS 1–17–1 Sendagaya, Shibuya-ku [1F 29]
STRUCTURAL ENGINEER Toshihiko Kimura Structural Engineers
CLIENT Tokyo Metropolitan Government
CONTRACTORS joint venture between Shimizu, Tokyu, Konoike, Dai Nippon, Katsunuma and Ogawa
SIZE 44,000 square metres
JR Sendagaya – Sobu Line
ACCESS open

Aoyama, Sendagaya

Fumihiko Maki & Associates 1990

Fumihiko Maki & Associates 1990

Hamlet

This 'temporal tent' houses three generations of a single family divided between four separate households. Each household is fully independent, though communication is facilitated by an infrastructure of exterior bridges, staircases and balconies. A basic unit, 3 metres wide, provides a building block from which different types of rooms can be assembled. Some units are connected to form a house.

The base of the structure is concrete and above this steel columns and truss beams support the walkways and awning roofs. This 'scaffolding' gives the impression of a building under construction. The white membrane spinnaker sails at the roof add to the image of transience.

The architect's priority was to meet the needs of the family rather than structural design. Appropriate relationships between individuals and groups, families and neighbours and private and public were carefully incorporated into the plan with the result that this is not a place for isolated modern individuals but an interactive neighbourhood. The design draws on the spatial hierarchies observed in studies of traditional communities around the Mediterranean.

Aoyama, Sendagaya

ADDRESS 4–20–8 Sendagaya, Shibuya-ku [1F 29]
STRUCTURAL ENGINEER SIGLO Engineering Associates
CONTRACTOR Nakano-Gumi Corporation
SIZE 561 square metres
JR Sendagaya – Chuo Line
ACCESS none

Riken Yamamoto and Field Shop 1988

Riken Yamamoto and Field Shop 1988

Terrazza

A solid concrete mass with three 38-metre towers houses a sports club for wealthy mid-lifers. Immense square openings in the heavy defensive façade reveal the depth of the walls, which are entirely plain except for dots and lines of moulded joints. This fortress protecting an exclusive inner sanctum is accessible through narrow interstices between the towers and steps which lead up the outside to a rooftop amphitheatre.

A 30-metre wall lying against the inside of the towers is angled oppressively over the entrance courtyard below. Here, the heavy stoicism of the open laid concrete captures something of the rough beauty of Roman outposts. Office space at the top is reached by a caged bridge suspended above the angled wall from the central tower, which contains a lift.

In the evening, lights are projected into the sky in a spectacular vision reminiscent of the 'walls of light' produced in Nazi Germany fifty years ago, while the towers resemble the massive concrete control towers erected in occupied Vienna – an architecture of triumphalism and theatre.

ADDRESS 2–8–2 Jingumae, Shibuya-ku [2G 29]
STRUCTURAL ENGINEER Pacific Consultants International
CONTRACTORS joint venture between Taisei and Dainihon-doboku
SIZE 6883 square metres
METRO Gaienmae – Ginza Line
ACCESS none

Aoyama, Sendagaya

Kiyoshi Sey Takeyama and Amorphe 1990

Aoyama, Sendagaya

United Arrows

This principal outlet of a leading fashion company, set well away from the main street in Japan's fashion district Harajuku, is patronised only by those in the know. The chosen theme was 'European-influenced design for the 1990s' and accordingly a Spanish architect, whose previous projects include Barcelona airport and a low-cost mansion block with palatial pretensions in a Parisian suburb, was selected. Bofill, working outside Europe for the first time and in typically chaotic Tokyo surroundings, decided an autonomous and strong design was essential. The result reflects his own interest in 'the union of classic and modern'.

A three-storey arcade of simplified European-style columns set along the entrance divides the building in two. The warm beige of the concrete derives from a blend of local Japanese sands. Shops set behind floor-to-ceiling sheet glass open on to this columned corridor on the left while opposite a structure of thin steel pipes supports glass behind which is a long straight staircase up to the third floor. Old and new are immaculately balanced and detailed.

Aoyama, Sendagaya

ADDRESS 3–28–1 Jingumae, Shibuya-ku [2G 29]
ASSOCIATED ARCHITECTS Kajima Design
CLIENT World, United Arrows
CONTRACTOR Kajima Corporation
SIZE 1305 square metres
JR Harajuku – Yamanote Line
ACCESS open

Ricardo Bofill 1992

Ricardo Bofill 1992

GA Gallery

Global Architecture is internationally renowned for its monthly magazine and architectural publications featuring sharply photographed buildings. The publisher and photographer Yukio Futagawa owns the gallery and bookshop on the lower floors of this much-visited centre for architects and GA's offices occupy the upper storeys.

The building, with its rough tactile concrete surfaces with traces of wooden shuttering, belongs to the 1970s' brutalist style. A gallery space is divided into two parts by a narrow interstice of glass.

Aoyama, Sendagaya

ADDRESS 3–12–16 Sendagaya, Shibuya-ku [2E 29]
SIZE 309 square metres
JR Sendagaya – Sobu Line
ACCESS open 10.00–18.00

Makoto Suzuki – AMS Architects 1983

Makoto Suzuki – AMS Architects 1983

Watari-um

There are many triangular sites along Tokyo's wider traffic-laden streets, relics of the often ill-considered, hectic city-planning that occurred during the period of rapid economic growth. Olympic Road, hurriedly constructed when Tokyo hosted the event in 1964, ploughed through the middle of a rectangular residential site set within a sleepy area of narrow medieval streets containing old wooden houses, temples and cemeteries. Another corner of the site lies on the opposite side of the street.

The Watari-um is a private museum owned by the Watari family, whose Galerie Watari gained a reputation for hosting consistently well-curated exhibitions. Previous exhibitors include Nam June Paik, Andy Warhol, Joseph Beuys, Buckminster Fuller and Keith Haring, as well as Swiss architect Mario Botta, whose reputation was later consolidated by a one-man show at Museum of Modern Art in New York.

The five-year design process of the Watari-um included a major battle against legal restrictions and, because the designation of the area was changed from residential to commercial as the building was under construction, the design of two different versions.

The contrast between the wide front street, now lined with modern buildings, and the area behind, packed with small two-storey houses and shops in a maze of narrow alleys, was an important issue for the architect: 'For this little museum, from the first drawings onwards, I followed a strong and precise image that had to resist the confusion and contradiction of languages, styles and forms present in Tokyo ... Tokyo exacerbates the contradictions of modern cities ... at every street corner, next to the lacerations inflicted by new planning developments, a dense urban context survives with a pre-industrial grid which offers a contrast between a spatial relationship and an urban memory.' (*Mario Botta: Watari-um Project in Tokyo*, author's translation.)

Aoyama, Sendagaya

Mario Botta 1990

In the end, the triangular site, 17 by 17 by 24 metres, proved ideal for Botta's main intention: 'geometric organisation of plan' and 'severe articulation of façades'. Walls are positioned as near as possible to the edges of the site. A circular lift shaft is set within the white-painted exhibition spaces, passing through ceiling slabs gridded with beams. Occasionally part of the ceiling slab is absent to allow for double-height spaces, producing a constant variation, floor by floor, within the tiny area. The exterior is densely banded with black granite and exposed concrete, making the 24-metre-high building appear taller than it is. An outdoor fire-escape stair at the south end, swinging out independently from the main symmetrical façade, gives the building a sharply angled edge.

ADDRESS 3–7–6 Jingumae, Shibuya-ku [2G 29]
CONTRACTOR Takenaka Corporation
SIZE 627 square metres
METRO Gaienmae – Ginza Line
ACCESS open 11.00–19.00

Mario Botta 1990

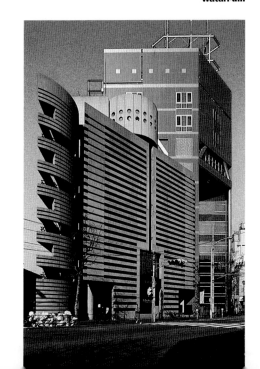

Aoyama Mihoncho

Nothing is on display in this shop apart from walls made up of thousands of slim Japanese oak drawers. Flooring throughout is brightly coloured, highly polished terrazzo tiles that reflect the small halogen lamps that run in lines down the ceiling. Minimalist furniture (counters, tables and chairs) is positioned at right angles and most of space is empty.

This is the shop of a well-established (since 1899) paper distributor and is patronised by many of the 800 design offices in the area. Mihoncho means 'sample file' and more than 4000 paper samples are available in the drawers, catalogued in an index which would-be purchasers consult. The atmosphere is not unlike that of a library reading room.

This system is a return to that of traditional Tokyo shops, in which merchandise – especially books and art works – was stored in drawers whose secrets were revealed by shopkeepers. Nothing was displayed and the feeling of personal service was all-important. This modern paper shop provides the flavour of shopping in former times, a leisurely art lost in today's unconstrained commercial age.

Aoyama, Sendagaya

ADDRESS 5–46–15 Jingumae, Shibuya-ku [4G 29]
CLIENT Takeo Company, Ltd
CONTRACTOR Build Company, Ltd
SIZE 103 square metres
METRO Omotesando – Chiyoda, Ginza, Hanzomon Line
ACCESS open 10.00–19.00

Shigeru Uchida and Studio 80 1989

Aoyama, Sendagaya

Metroça

The architect's concern was with the impossibility of designing architecture that would contribute meaningfully to a sense of 'city' in vast, elusive, constantly changing Tokyo. So from the outset, the idea of a façade – the most typical architectural statement – was abandoned and this residential mansion was to be constructed below ground. In the end, Kitagawara managed to fit in only half of the planned four storeys below street level, leaving two floors above. The plain lateral walls that take the place of façades appear undesigned and have a decadent beauty.

A thick concrete structural frame runs the height of the building into which walls of different materials defining different rooms are inserted. Apparently random layers on the north-western side – a pink mortar wall, glass, the main concrete frame and a white steel-mesh screen – are revealed behind a white plaster wall and a curving black steel panel. On the south-western side, a grey mortar wall and the main concrete frame stand beside a metal fence made up of 40 stainless-steel strips connected by small angled cross-bars. This screens the basement courtyard, seductively floored with stainless steel with a white pitched tent and stairs that suggest an architectural incident.

Aoyama, Sendagaya

ADDRESS 5–40–10 Jingumae, Shibuya-ku [4G 29]
STRUCTURAL ENGINEER Ikea Structure Design Office
CONTRACTOR Construction Company, Ltd
SIZE 499 square metres
METRO Omotesando–Chiyoda, Ginza, Hanzomon Line
ACCESS none

Atsushi Kitagawara + ILCD 1989

Aoyama, Sendagaya

Atsushi Kitagawara + ILCD 1989

Philo Aoyama

The 'skipping' floors and twisting steps inside this three-storey building can be seen through a large window in the façade. From the open entrance space, two sets of steps lead to a ground floor set a little higher than street level and to a lower level. Imported gifts and household goods are piled high, luring you in both directions.

The interior is simple with different materials defining the walls, floor and ceiling. A mortar wall on the right leads customers towards the stacked shelves at the rear; the other walls are painted white. The cherry-wood shelving continues along the left wall, and before you have a chance to escape this tempting bazaar, a flight of stairs at the centre leads you up to the mezzanine.

Here one turns again and the ceiling, made of light brown particle board, sweeps over in a curve before shooting towards the sky, which is framed by a wide glass window at the top.

ADDRESS 5–49–2 Jingumae, Shibuya-ku [4G 29]
STRUCTURAL ENGINEER TIS & Partners
CLIENT Fujii Kosan Company, Ltd
CONTRACTOR Matsui Construction, Build Company, Ltd
SIZE 308 square metres
METRO Omotesando – Chiyoda, Ginza, Hanzomon Line
ACCESS Monday–Saturday 11.00–19.00

Aoyama, Sendagaya

Katsuhiko Togashi 1993

Katsuhiko Togashi 1993

United Nations University

The elder architect continues his post-modern themes in an out-scaled and heavily symmetrical design, clad with stone panels. If his Tokyo City Hall is compared to Notre-Dame in Paris, this could be the Duomo in Milan. Thus, his recent designs tend to be at the 'gothic' end of this century's 'post-neo-classic-modernism'.

This is the only United Nations facility with a headquarters in Japan and, in spite of the name, it has no students. Instead, it functions as a core for international networking of the many areas of study concerning 'development, continuation and welfare of Man on earth'. Tange's aim was to establish the appropriate majesty and symbolic authority for this egalitarian facility for world peace.

Everything is designed to emphasise the main axis and it follows that the highest point of the skyline comes at the dead centre of the façade. The first-storey height is significantly elevated but rather too humbling for its peaceful intention. As you promenade fashionable Aoyama-dori street, passing other more sympathetic developments, strong winds blow around the threatening façade across a vast open plaza at the front.

Aoyama, Sendagaya

ADDRESS 5–53–1 Jingumae, Shibuya-ku [4G 29]
STRUCTURAL ENGINEER Takumi Orimoto & Associates
CLIENT Ministry of Education
CONTRACTOR joint venture of Kajima, Nishimatsu, Hazama, Tokai, Aoki
SIZE 21,300 square metres
METRO Omotesando – Chiyoda, Ginza, Hanzomon Line
ACCESS none

Kenzo Tange Associates 1992

Aoyama, Sendagaya

Kenzo Tange Associates 1992

Shibuya

Tanabe Agency

Can there be architectural jokes? Is it necessary for architects to be serious or sober about architecture?

The question was an important one for the architect who was commissioned to design this building for a theatrical agent who has promoted many of the popular comedians and media stars of the past decade. Tanabe, the head of the agency, suggested that humour lies in the impure and unexpected; the juxtaposition or cross-breeding of unlikely pairs. So the architect created a seemingly incongruous hybrid: an office building that is a 'bridge' between comedy and architecture.

Ishii, who studied under American post-modernist Charles Moore, is well known for his irreverent architecture and mocking assemblages of quotations. But his buildings are consistently well designed and this bridge is no exception. The plan is a simple rectangle with a circular glass-block staircase at the centre. The structure uses glass walls to their full advantage to create an open and light interior. The salon at the top is furnished with Le Corbusier chairs, reinforcing the sense of a stylish establishment for the famous to relax in.

ADDRESS 2–21–4 Aobadai, Meguro-ku [4C 22]
CONTRACTOR Sato Hide Construction
SIZE 530 square metres
RAIL Nakameguro – Tokyu Toyoko Line
ACCESS none

Shibuya

Kazuhiro Ishii 1984

Shibuya

Earth Tecture sub-1

Shin Takamatsu admits: 'I am very apprehensive about whether or not to call this mysterious structure a piece of architecture.' And indeed, its cryptic character makes it unlike any other building, even in Tokyo.

Takamatsu sees architecture not just as a functional container for living and working, but as an entity which possesses an autonomous power. For a thousand years Kyoto, his native city, was the capital of Japan, and many of its surviving historic buildings have a strong aura of past power struggles, glory and decline, and these presences are explored.

With the full support of his client, Takamatsu intended to build something that, while remaining within the bounds of contemporary urban architecture, would exceed, or rather disregard, the usual constraints of function and cost. 'The programme may have included the acquisition of the maximum practical volume of space, but it also comprised the more important points of establishing a notably high presence and stressing the individuality of the architecture itself.'(Shin Takamatsu, *JA Library*)

All four floors of the 'building' are underground and only three emblematic towers indicate its presence. These are, in fact, elaborate skylights through which natural light falls into a quarter-circle void down to the lower basements. Each of these is a quarter segment of a sphere. At the top of each curve spring pairs of steel rods, or insect-like antennae. The frames for the glass are arranged in a striking radial design similar to the symbol of the rising sun that adorns the flag of the Imperial Japanese Navy. Located in a largely residential area, these forms are encountered as strange and surprising.

As one steps through the entrance and peers down to the base of the deep 'well', a disconcerting sense of vertigo sets in.

The surrounding land is landscaped as a kind of 'Elysian fields': walls of bamboo and a 'ground' of polished black granite are laid around the

Shin Takamatsu 1991

Shibuya

Shin Takamatsu 1991

metallic quarter-sphere roofs of the 'towers'. The role of the façade is displaced: there are no walls to divide inside from outside or to communicate to passers-by the function and layout of the interior, but instead a frame around the site which separates it from its surroundings.

This very experimental project may turn out to have a short life due to its unprofitability. Its ruin would leave a trace of a small transgressive dream.

ADDRESS 2–29–3 Uehara, Shibuya-ku [5D 28]
STRUCTURAL ENGINEER Yamamoto-Tachibana
Architects & Engineers
CLIENT Green Homes Corporation
CONTRACTOR Konoike-gumi Construction
SIZE 455 square metres
METRO Yoyogi-Uehara – Chiyoda Line
ACCESS open

Shin Takamatsu 1991

Gallery TOM

It is misleading to represent this building visually, while its mass, materials and volumes cannot appropriately be described in words. 'Touch Our Museum' is a gallery designed and built for blind people.

The gallery owner, a constructivist sculptor, lives on the ground floor. The entrance is situated on the second floor – or more precisely at the fifteenth step of the widening stairs with their wooden handrails. Push open a cool glass door and you encounter sculptures set on a waist-height wooden shelf. Touch and explore the forms and your hands will lead you around the gallery. The tall space is planned to exploit the acoustics and sunlight, which passes through a glass and steel-beam-slatted roof-light to stimulate the skin. The shelf becomes a handrail to the third floor and finally leads you to the fresh breezes of the terrace.

Sight, you are reminded, is only one of five senses by which architecture is experienced.

ADDRESS 2–11–1 Shoto, Shibuya-ku [5E 28]
STRUCTURAL ENGINEER Kunio Watanabe/Structural Design Group Company, Ltd
CONTRACTOR Shiraishi Construction Company, Ltd
SIZE 250 square metres
JR Shibuya – Yamanote Line
RAIL Shinsen – Keio Inokashira Line
ACCESS open Tuesday–Sunday, 10.30–17.30

Shibuya

Hiroshi Naito 1984

Shibuya

Hiroshi Naito 1984

Setsu-getsu-ka

The interior of this restaurant is fanatically minimal, without a single awkward corner or protruding detail. All the surfaces are flat and the edges are blade sharp. The lighting, arranged in lines down the length of the ceiling, throws out a clean brightness. Mizutani thinks of design in terms of lit volumes – that is, the volume is engendered by the manipulation of light and shade.

The dramatic space is divided into three areas: Setsu, a Kaiseki restaurant serving small, beautifully arranged dishes; Getsu, a French restaurant; and Ka, a bar. The client, who is from Kyoto, wanted something representative of the style of his native city but with a modern emphasis, so Japanese wallpaper and cypress wood are incorporated into the fabric of the space.

ADDRESS B1F Royal Palace Harajuku, 1–5–4 Jinnan, Shibuya-ku [4F 29]
CONTRACTOR Inter-Design Company
SIZE 166 square metres
JR Shibuya – Yamanote Line
ACCESS open Monday to Saturday, 11.00–14.00, 17.30–24.00

Shibuya

Soshi Mizutani 1992

Shibuya

Soshi Mizutani 1992

Shibuya Beam

On Friday nights the maze of streets here heaves with revellers: 'first-date' couples, rowdy adolescents, drunken 'salary men'. A myriad of bars, cinemas, restaurants, techno-games centres, pachinko parlours, discount shops and the ubiquitous department stores, all with neon displays, supply a flashy upbeat dream designed to thrill young hearts and entice full wallets. Shibuya is a thriving commercial centre that grew in tandem with the economic boom of past ten years. Shibuya Beam lies at its centre.

The seven-storey building plus three basement floors contains karaoke bars, amusement arcades, restaurants and a 'promotion' theatre directly accessible from the street where companies present images of their latest products for downmarket consumers. The design consists of a meaningless selection of elements from other Shibuya buildings. The theatre is enclosed by a curved white wall. Floors are hung from concrete walls on thick tension rods in a cheap imitation of British high-tech. A hemispherical glass dome at the top encloses a conservatory restaurant.

Shibuya Beam is a prime example of the unashamed commercialism that makes up the area's culture.

ADDRESS 31–2 Udagawa-cho, Shibuya-ku [5F 29]
STRUCTURAL ENGINEERS Ikeda Structure Design Office and Tokyu Architects & Engineers
CLIENT Tokyu Land Corporation
CONTRACTOR Tokyu Construction
SIZE 11,340 square metres
JR Shibuya – Yamanote Line
ACCESS public spaces are open

Workshop 1992

Workshop 1992

Fuji Building 40

The area around Shibuya Station is distinguished by a complex layered junction of highways, pedestrian overpasses and overhead railways that compete for airspace and head off in every direction through and past department stores and grimy eateries. A pedestrian bridge crosses an eight-lane river of fast-flowing traffic and ducks below a heavy concrete highway before reaching the relative calm of the steep hillside that rises above.

Fuji Building Company has been trying for some time to develop the Sakuragaoka-cho district into an office area and has already started a building programme. No. 40 is intended as a gateway to and precedent for the upgraded area.

The façade is made up of glass walls with stepped upper sections that create outside terraces. Double- and triple-height volumes behind the glazing accentuate the spaciousness of the open-plan floors, which look out over the narrow abyss of the 3.5-metre-wide street. Space is available – but be prepared to come up with ¥36 billion per month, plus a ¥1700 billion deposit.

ADDRESS 15–14 Sakuragaoka-cho, Shibuya-ku [5G 29]
STRUCTURAL ENGINEER Ascoral Engineering Associates
CONTRACTOR Shimizu Corporation
SIZE 4660 square metres
JR Shibuya – Yamanote Line
ACCESS none

Shibuya

Kojiro Kitayama 1992

Shibuya

Kojiro Kitayama 1992

Bunkamura

Bunkamura means 'Cultural Village'. Tokyu Corporation, the developer, is primarily a railway company with a strong base in Shibuya, where it owns the Tokyu Toyoko Line and eight department stores. Its rival railway company Seibu has recently expanded its share in Shibuya to eight department stores, so this ninth flagship building represents the latest round of an intensely fought competition and hopefully, for Tokyu, the final word.

The target customers are the culturally minded. A narrow 32,000-square-metre space at the rear of an existing Tokyu Department Store contains a 2,150-seat symphony hall (the Orchard Hall), the 747-seat Theatre Cocoon, a museum and various shops, cafés and restaurants.

The main entrance lobby, an inner court, a bookshop and a restaurant are fine examples of the work of French interior designer Jean-Michel Wilmotte. The bright, ordered, and not overly extravagant aesthetic has a distinct sense of 'Parisian chic', a term which quickly became the commercial catchphrase for the project.

ADDRESS 2–24–1 Dogenzaka, Shibuya-ku [5F 29]
CLIENT Tokyu Department Store
SIZE 32,000 square metres
JR Shibuya – Yamanote Line
ACCESS open 10.00–21.30

Shibuya

Jean-Michel Wilmotte Japon/Ishimoto Architects & Engineers 1989

Jean-Michel Wilmotte Japon/Ishimoto Architects & Engineers 1989

Humax Pavilion Shibuya

Koen-dori Street provides the launch site for a sensational and highly decorative rocket. Humax, an entertainment development company, has built a complex of cinemas, restaurants and discotheques leading off a central circular hall topped by a glass nose-cone which houses a restaurant. Fins or flying buttresses and thin vertical tubular columns are overlaid on the façade, lending the structure a Gothic air, while the combination of dark stone cladding and metallic elements is distinctly Art Deco.

But in spite of the architect's efforts to differentiate the building from the surrounding fashion shops and department stores, it barely makes an impact. One could easily pass it by if it weren't for the ultra-bright Disney merchandise shop on the ground floor for which it provides an appropriate home.

ADDRESS 20–15 Udagawa-cho, Shibuya-ku [5F 29]
STRUCTURAL ENGINEER Numao Architects
CLIENT Humax
CONTRACTOR Kumagaya Construction
SIZE 4500 square metres
JR Shibuya – Yamanote Line
ACCESS open (some facilities are members only)

Hiroyuki Wakabayashi 1992

Shibuya

Hiroyuki Wakabayashi 1992

Aoyama Technical College

This bizarre apparition is a school, not a science-fiction creature out to destroy the city. The initial response to a close encounter is usually 'What is that?', followed by 'How on earth... ?' The architect's first work, it defies any step-by-step description.

In fact, each of the seemingly arbitrary design elements is there for a purpose. The architect set himself the task of analysing the 'self-organisation' of Tokyo's urban systems and then simulated the process on his drawing board: 'They are all essential architectural elements – posts, water tanks, lightning rod, joints of various kinds. But these parts, after fulfilling their required functions, maintain the momentum of growth, rising up like so many flourishing young shoots. If they all continued to grow arbitrarily, friction would arise among them, causing the collapse of the whole. So the growing parts begin spontaneously to adjust their relationships to one another and to alter themselves accordingly.'

Is Tokyo as monstrous as Watanabe's vision would have us believe?

ADDRESS 7–9 Uguisudani, Shibuya-ku [5G 29]
CONTRACTOR Konoike-gumi Construction
SIZE 1480 square metres
JR Shibuya – Yamanote Line
ACCESS only by booking in advance;
telephone 03-3463-0901

Shibuya

Makoto Sei Watanabe / Architects' Office 1990

Shibuya

Makoto Sei Watanabe / Architects' Office 1990

Hillside Terrace

This complex is possibly unique in that a single architect was invited to develop different parts of a street over a period of nearly a quarter of a century. Although covering a relatively small area, the design has a force and integrity which have influenced new building in the entire Daikan-yama district. From the initial project to the latest sixth stage, the styles and materials have changed, reflecting the passage of time and Maki's own maturing tastes and concerns. The basic programme is simple: shops and restaurants on the ground floor and apartments above.

Daikanyama is a peaceful, exclusive residential area at the top of a hill, as the latter part of the name, *yama* (mountain), suggests. Lush greenery, garden walls and private houses line the pavements, creating an environment suitable for strolling in. The client, the Asakura family, owns the land along Kyu-Yamate-dori Street, which defines the edge of the 'upper' town.

Maki's urban philosophy is based on the idea that until the 19th century, places all over the world had their own specific cultures and architectural forms, but since the middle of this century, under the name of 'modernisation', this individuality has been gradually eroded. Inhabitants' lack of understanding of their own cityscapes has led to a loss of meaning. In addition, media saturation has produced longings for a fictional 'country-ness' or 'foreignness' that bears little relation to what the reality of 'country' or 'foreign' might be.

The main theme of Maki's development here is therefore the 're-construction of the city's changing vista'. A simple but sophisticated chain of buildings is set against a background of twisting pathways. Though there are no traditional features on any of buildings, the scale and the combination of volume and void draw on the surrounding environment, while the mass of the whole is reduced through the juxtaposi-

Fumihiko Maki & Associates 1969–92

Shibuya

Fumihiko Maki & Associates 1969–92

tion of a number of smaller volumes. As you walk through the complexes, you are offered a series of different perspectives, while the transparent walls link the paths outside to the white spaces of the interiors.

The earliest development, the A and B complex, is at the eastern end of the site. A transparent lobby, sunken garden and pedestrian deck provide the base for two white cubes of maisonettes.

The second development, C complex, continues a similar theme adapted to the wider depth of the site by a plaza set behind the streetside volume with a further addition at the back. The increased traffic meant that both developments were subsequently sprayed with a special white paint to protect them from car exhaust fumes.

The third development, D and E complex, is tiled with white porcelain and built around Sarugakuzuka, an ancient mound with a tiny shrine at its crest. This green enclosure complements the intimate mood of the public pathways. In 1979 the Danish Embassy, also designed by Maki, was added to complete the 200 metres of streetside development with a pink tiled curved wall.

The fourth development, annex A and B, consists of two concrete buildings set behind the A complex. These were designed by Makoto Motokura, who took charge of the project under Maki's supervision. The fifth development, a multi-purpose hall, is below ground beneath the parking lots between B and C complexes.

The sixth and latest development, F and G buildings (six and four storeys respectively), is on the opposite side of the street. The third-floor canopy lines reflect the height of the buildings opposite and the higher floors are set back. A small courtyard between the two buildings, planted with elegant plane trees, provides a lead-in to a set-back gallery. One passes through the entrance to encounter a further small open court situ-

Fumihiko Maki & Associates 1969–92

Shibuya

Fumihiko Maki & Associates 1969–92

ated inside the building. Here a clean white space contains a shallow pool within which is an artwork – a wall that can be read from either side. The window side of the gallery provides the location for a café and a chic spot to pause between shopping and absorbing some culture over a cappuccino

The glass-walled areas on the ground and second levels give the scheme a luminous quality, while a steel frame at the corner of the second floor of the F building means the box remains unenclosed. The sharp edge details and aluminium panels contribute to the sophisticated sense of lightness.

ADDRESS 29–8 Sarugaku-cho, Shibuya-ku [6G 29]
CLIENT Asakura Real Estate Company, Ltd
CONTRACTOR Takenaka Corporation
SIZE 17,700 square metres
BUILT 1st 1969, 2nd 1973, 3rd 1977, 4th 1985, 5th 1987, 6th 1992
RAIL Daikanyama – Tokyu Toyoko Line
ACCESS open

Fumihiko Maki & Associates 1969–92

Shibuya

Shinagawa

Unhex Nani-Nani

This, the French designer Philippe Starck's second building in Tokyo, has been described by him as 'a green monster [that] came out from marshy Florida'. The latter part of the name, which translates as 'what?-what?', was apparently inspired by the confusion experienced by the various parties during the building process.

The unsettling anthropomorphic form of the steel-structured five-storey office building is clad in green copper panels. Thin bands of window relieve the solidity of the south-facing end, but the rest of the building is windowless.

This forbidding entity is located in a sunny tree-lined street, an incongruous insertion among the conventional villas. The beauty of the copper lightens the contrast.

ADDRESS 4–9–23 Shirokanedai, Minato-ku [6F 9]
ASSOCIATED ARCHITECTS Makoto Nozawa and GETT
CLIENT Rikugo Construction
CONTRACTOR Rikugo Construction
SIZE 720 square metres
JR Meguro – Yamanote Line
ACCESS none

Shinagawa

Philippe Starck 1989

Shinagawa

Philippe Starck 1989

Tokyo Design Centre

An Italian architect was presented with a challenging site on which to erect a centre for interior design. By avoiding the more central arts-oriented areas such as Aoyama and Roppongi in favour of the southern end of Yamanote, where land is relatively cheap, a much larger centre could be built. The complex – nine storeys high with two basement floors – is an easily distinguished landmark from Sakurada-dori and the nearby JR train line.

Bellini had to cope with two major obstacles. First, a building with a dull 1970s' façade occupied the prime streetside location at the centre of the site, making it impossible to design a continuous frontage. Second, 'off-site shadow control' regulations required the building to slope sharply down at the rear, restricting the depth of the upper floors. As a result, the complex is continuous at the rear but divided in two at the front, making a 'C' shape.

Each wing has a distinctive pyramidal roof to reinforce the idea that the two parts of the façade make up a pair. The stepped terraces at the rear are topped with giant flower-pots and have views of a temple on higher ground. This calm environment is an effective contrast with the busy street.

The split façade is made of concrete with Italian travertine lines or 'joints'. What appear to be shutters at the tall windows are in fact concrete walls which project through to the outside. The taller height, overbearing weight of the walls and relatively plain design distinguish the building from its neighbours. The architect rightly anticipated that 'silence' would be the most effective way to give the complex a presence against the 'noisy' background of Tokyo.

The main entrance is situated at the southern wing. A gap, five storeys high, is divided by an inserted travertine wall that cuts diagonally through

Shinagawa

Mario Bellini 1992

Shinagawa

Mario Bellini 1992

the building to the rear. At the end of the resultant galleria can be seen a sculpture of a horse; placed at the head of two flights of elegant steps, and framed against the light, this is intended to entice people inside. This tall narrow space acts as a core for circulation, connecting front and back. Wide doorways lead to other parts of the building and the space is crossed by bridges. A café, design bookshop and multi-purpose hall are also included.

ADDRESS 5–25–19 Higashi-gotanda, Shinagawa-ku [2D 20]
ASSOCIATED ARCHITECTS Obayashi Corporation
CLIENT Sowa-Shoji Corporation
CONTRACTOR Obayashi Corporation
SIZE 11,370 square metres
JR Gotanda – Yamanote Line
ACCESS open

Mario Bellini 1992

Shinagawa

Mario Bellini 1992

House F

This fairly typical modern suburban house is distinguished by its unusual roof. Irregularly sized triangular planes are assembled to form an undulating lightweight sheet that is structurally independent of the walls. The continuous glazed windows around the upper parts of the rear walls and extending the full height of the upper storey at the front cause the roof to appear to float. Inside, the foliage of the surrounding trees is visible through the 'gap', so the living area seems to expand beyond its physical boundary.

This effect is made possible by a combination of two different structures. The rooms are enclosed by reinforced-concrete walls, while independent steel columns extend from the ground level to the third floor. Rods pin-jointed at the top of each of these columns are triangulated to create a space-truss to which the roof appears tethered.

Shinagawa

ADDRESS Koyama, Shinagawa-ku [5A 20]
STRUCTURAL ENGINEER Dan Engineering
SIZE 172 square metres
RAIL Senzoku – Tokyu Mekama Line
ACCESS none

Kazunari Sakamoto 1988

Shinagawa

Kazunari Sakamoto 1988

Polygon Pictures

A young and progressive company producing high-tech computer graphics invited a fashionable interior designer to create a trendy, 'mechanical-looking' office in a warehouse near a Tokyo waterfront with the unlikely name of Bond Street. The storeroom office is 7 by 20 metres with a lofty 4.5-metre-high ceiling in which the designer erected a dramatic double-height structural frame, 6 by 14 metres, made up of red-painted steel beams on a 1.8-metre grid.

A manager's office is located on the upper floor of the frame and the stairs are tensioned by thin cables. Fluorescent lights are hung on a further framework made of thin steel pipes and rods which throws a network of shadows across the white ceiling. The black office furniture and flooring provide an effective contrast.

ADDRESS 6th floor, T–11 Bond Street, 2–2–43 Higashi-shinagawa, Shinagawa-ku [2F 21]
CONTRACTOR Build Company, Ltd
SIZE 215 square metres
JR Shinagawa – Yamanote Line
ACCESS none

Shinagawa

Yasuo Kondo 1987

Shinagawa

Yasuo Kondo 1987

Meguro Gajoen

A hotel and office complex covers a 30,000-square-metre site alongside the River Meguro. The extensive riverside façades of the two buildings are clad in small porcelain tiles of five hues – ranging from grey to light blue – that give the structures an iridescent glow.

The nineteen-storey office building has continuous bands of tinted glass that reflect the sky and a helicopter pad on the roof adds to the building's high-flying lines. Inside, the walls and ceiling of the 100-metre lobby are panelled in black-and-white book-leafed marble.

The hotel should only be described only in superlatives – most fabulous, splendid … It provides the backdrop for many a dreamboat wedding and a total of 24 happy occasions can take place simultaneously. The smaller suites cater for up to fifty guests and the largest for 1000. There is a huge choice of traditional or western-style rooms, a Christian chapel and a Shinto shrine – whatever your religion or preferred setting, it can be catered for, no problem. Super-weddings have become a growth industry over the past decade and sumptuous, eye-popping venues such as this are widely advertised.

The hotel replaces the former Gajoen, built at the beginning of the century. Familiarly known as 'Ryugu-jo' or 'fairytale dragon palace', it was filled with over 5000 painted reliefs of traditional scenes of women. Half this collection has been restored and relocated in the new building, along with sculptures and other antiques from the original. Many of these are displayed in a ground-floor corridor, nearly 200 metres long, laid out like a museum. Continuous glass walling provides views of a formal garden and a bubbling stream meanders in and out.

This gallery forms a dramatic approach to the vast central four-storey glass atrium, which houses an entire traditional wooden building (a restaurant) complete with thatched roof and bamboo and rock garden.

Nikken Sekkei, Ltd 1991

Shinagawa

Barely a mossy-stone's throw away, bridal couples descend a curving Hollywood-style staircase to be captured on the camcorders of their guests below. From here it is but a short step outside for more photo calls on a wooden bridge in front of a magnificent sheet waterfall. All this extravagance is mitigated by the meticulously harmonious detailing, which gives the hotel an impressive air of top-notch quality.

ADDRESS 1–8–1 Shimo-meguro, Meguro-ku [ID 22]
CONTRACTOR Kajima Corporation
CONTRACT VALUE ¥80 billion
SIZE 134,550 square metres
JR Meguro – Yamanote Line
ACCESS open

Shinagawa

Nikken Sekkei, Ltd 1991

Nikken Sekkei, Ltd 1991

Shinjuku

New Tokyo City Hall Complex

The purpose of this design was to produce a landmark to represent the authority of the Tokyo metropolitan government and to provide a home for its vast bureaucratic machine. It was on completion the tallest building in Tokyo and 13,000 people work in the 400,000 square metres of space. The site of the former city hall, also designed by Kenzo Tange, is currently being redeveloped as the Tokyo International Forum (see page 58).

Tange's visionary design was chosen over more conventional high-rise office buildings submitted to the 1986 competition because of its symbolic appearance and highly formalised planning. The other main contender was Arata Isozaki's remarkable 'low-rise' proposal (only 23 storeys high and 300 metres long), presented as an alternative to and criticism of hierarchical representations. Some critics felt that Isozaki's project was better, but that the outcome of the competition may have been prejudiced by the fact that during the election for the leader of the metropolitan government, Tange, a highly respected establishment figure, had openly supported the re-selection of Suzuki as governor of Tokyo.

The area on which the complex stands was formerly occupied by a water purification plant that once supplied all of Tokyo. The large empty tract of land at the heart of the city provided a unique planning opportunity. Other high-rise offices built there during the 1970s and early 1980s, each occupying an entire block and unusually tall for this earthquake-prone city, were likened by some to 'urban tombstones'. Three blocks at the centre of the site were reserved for Tokyo's flagship, and Tange took advantage of the wide area to create a strongly symmetrical design around a central axis that runs through the main building.

This has forty-eight floors set within twin 243-metre-high towers. The tops of these towers are rotated 45 degrees, lending the static bulk a twisting upwards motion, while the central lower section between is set

Shinjuku

Kenzo Tange Associates 1991

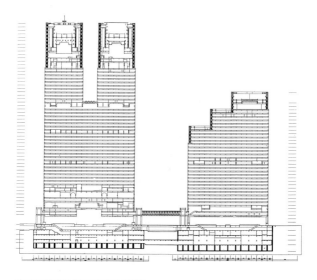

Kenzo Tange Associates 1991

Shinjuku

slightly back. This format has associations with a 'cathedral of the state'.

In comparison with the visually complex exterior, the plan is simple. Four service cores, 6.4 metres square, at the corners of each of the towers function as columns which run the full height of the building, supported horizontally by two beams on each floor and main truss beams on the sixteenth and twenty-fifth floors. This gives 20 by 100 metres of column-free space throughout, allowing for flexible planning. The twist in the towers is produced by the simple strategy of changing the window-side wall between the columns. A grid pattern of granite panels of two colours combined with dark glass, stainless-steel maintenance bars and aluminium panels produces a dense 'integrated circuit-board' mass of details over the vast façade.

Across the street, steps lead down to a sunken semi-oval European-style plaza with columns and statues. An eight-storey building sweeps around this and continues back over the street in the form of two narrow bridges to the main building. At the top of this smaller building, above a massive portal set on the central axis of the complex, is an oval assembly hall. The plaza acts like the pit of a theatre, in which public officials can be glimpsed striding to and from meetings. A further building on the southern side of the complex uses the same features and materials. Here three towers of different heights (the highest has thirty-four floors) step down to the central axis.

When Tange's 'Notre-Dame' design was published, many architects criticised the master of modernism's espousal of post-modern symbolism, while others disliked the overtones of totalitarianism in the design, deemed entirely inappropriate for a government body of a liberal democratic country. Journalists from the tabloid newspapers hounded the governor about rumours that his office adjoined a luxury shower fitted

Kenzo Tange Associates 1991

out in marble. Perhaps more comically disturbing is the position of his office: on the seventh floor at the centre of the twin-towered building, it looks out across the plaza. Here an imperial-style balcony might foreseeably provide a spot for waving to a gathered populace against a monumental backdrop.

But public buildings of this scale always invite controversy, and in the end Tange's scheme evidently fulfils its brief. The building is well known throughout Tokyo and the viewing room on the forty-fifth floor was visited by nearly 2.5 million people in both 1991 and 1992, an average of 6000 a day.

ADDRESS 2–8–1 Nishi-shinjuku, Shinjuku-ku [5E 10]
STRUCTURAL ENGINEER Mutoh Associates
CONTRACT VALUE ¥157 billion
SIZE 380,000 square metres
JR Shinjuku – Yamanote Line
METRO Shinjuku – Marunouchi Line
ACCESS open; a guided tour is available by booking in advance: telephone 03-5321-1111

Kenzo Tange Associates 1991

Shinjuku

Kenzo Tange Associates 1991

Sticks

For architect Takeo Kimura, the environment of Tokyo is impossible to ignore. While others may design buildings evoking Utopian ideals, he explores issues generated by the chaotic city. His buildings aim to present 'not quotations from the past or future, but from the present.' Existing systems, contexts and codes are re-examined: 'Tokyo, not as a city composed of many buildings on plots of the smallest conceivable dimensions, but as a city integrated from innumerable, various and different details which are never unified.'

This eight-storey office building stands near the Sotobori (the Imperial Palace's outer moat) and is typical in that it looks on to an elevated highway and has small buildings behind. According to the architect, it bows to neither side but is rather a 'part' produced by a simulation of the fragmented 'whole', a stave planted that is both dividing and disconnecting. Standard modern design details are collaged together: Japanese-style *mengoshi* (flat gridded frame), curtain wall, fire-prevention walls and the external walls of the multi-storey car park. A steel fire-escape is revealed on the main façade. A curved glass wall, angled outwards with each floor, is set with elongated mullions – the 'sticks' from which the building takes its name. A square box with ordered windows has been added to the the north side, and aluminium bars slatted over the wall.

ADDRESS 1–14 Ogawa-cho, Shinjuku-ku [1J 11]
STRUCTURAL ENGINEER Ikeda Sekkei, Ltd
CONTRACTOR Tekken Corporation
SIZE 1670 square metres
JR Iidabashi – Chuo Line
METRO Iidabashi – Yurakucho Line
ACCESS none

Shinjuku

TAO Architects 1992

TAO Architects 1992

Obunsha Headquarters

These two five-storey buildings, the new headquarters for a publishing company, are not easily distinguishable as the work of Norman Foster. They are located in a narrow street crowded with many other types of building and were 'designed' more by legal and economic restrictions than anything else. Built towards the end of the period of fast economic growth, the client's requirements were trimmed down. The high price of the land demanded an economically efficient investment and restrictions on volume and height determined the buildings' profile.

The ceiling height, 2.45 metres, is too low for the open plan and the interior spaces are no different from those of other Tokyo 'economy' offices. Only the simple glazed façades and white double-height entrance halls reveal the signature of the architect.

ADDRESS 55 Yokodera-cho, Shinjuku-ku [21 11]
STRUCTURAL ENGINEER Obayashi Corporation
CLIENT Obunsha Pacific Corporation
CONTRACTOR Obayashi Corporation
SIZE 4907 and 4781 square metres
METRO Kagurazaka – Tozai Line
ACCESS none

Sir Norman Foster & Partners 1993

Sir Norman Foster & Partners 1993

Kabuki-cho Building

To date only one building by the influential British architect Sir Richard Rogers can be included in this book. Several more Tokyo projects were under development, but sadly these have not been completed since the clients suffered heavy losses following the collapse of the bubble economy. And this building is so badly located, in a back street of an insalubrious area, that it has not provided the triumphant Tokyo debut Rogers deserved.

At the end of the Second World War, Kabuki-cho became the centre of the black-market economy (a fragment of this post-war slum still remains as the Golden-gai) and before that it was known as a cheap brothel area. Today, underground culture continues to thrive despite regular police clampdowns: peep-show parlours, hostess bars, 'no-panties' coffee shops and 'Soaplands' are crowded into narrow streets among a panoply of neon, music, noisy announcements, bars and cinemas. 'Salary men' and young hippies wander the sleazy streets which are patrolled by pimps and Yakuzas (Japan's Mafia). It is said that the area provided inspiration for the sets in Ridley Scott's *Blade Runner*.

Rogers' ten-storey office building is located at the eastern end of Kabuki-cho. It fronts on to a street barely wide enough for a car, making it difficult to see or appreciate it. However, a delicate yacht-like tension structure immediately catches the eye. A framework of stainless-steel rods supports a slanting glazed roof over a deep basement space between the street and the main part of the building.

As you look up to see the whole building, the 'kit of parts' assemblage comes into view. The verticality of the lift, stairs and other services is, as usual, emphasised. Emergency exit units are coloured yellow and the blue staircase, assembled with beautiful joint details and no welding, is suspended by wires from an upper frame. The glazed façade has sun blinds

Richard Rogers Partnership 1993

Richard Rogers Partnership 1993

which are rolled out and unrolled automatically by light sensors.

A reinforced-concrete frame, thickened and solid to resist earthquakes, provides the main structure, preventing the Rogers practice from pursuing the structural developments for which it is perhaps best known.

ADDRESS 2–1–6 Kabuki-cho, Shinjuku-ku [4F 11]
ASSOCIATED ARCHITECT Architect Five Partnership
STRUCTURAL ENGINEER Umezawa Design Office
CONTRACTOR Kawata Kogyo
SIZE 1760 square metres
JR Shinjuku –Yamanote Line
ACCESS none

Shinjuku

Richard Rogers Partnership 1993

Shinjuku

New National Theatre

Takahiko Yanagisawa won first prize for this design in a 1986 competition, triumphing over opposition that included Bernard Tschumi, Peter Eisenman and Hans Hollein. But the completion date has been postponed several times and major planning adjustments were needed after a tall Inter-Communication Center tower containing a hypermedia museum was built on adjacent land. Unless further delays arise, the theatre will open early in 1997.

The 2.8-hectare site will house a new centre for the promotion of the contemporary stage arts. A long low building will contain seven rehearsal halls and three theatres which are claimed to have the best acoustics in the world. The main theatre for opera and ballet will seat nearly 2000, a medium-sized theatre with 1000 seats will stage modern drama, and a small theatre will be used primarily for experimental works.

Outside public spaces are organised as an 'open theatre', mediating between the noisy surroundings and nearby elevated highway and the introversion of the stage. A water cascade, pond and high promenade wall are set among glazed roofs and glass walls enclosing wide stairs, creating what the architect describes as 'dramatic tension to draw visitors out of the "ordinary world" and into an extra-ordinary world'.

Shinjuku

ADDRESS 1–1 Hon-machi, Shibuya-ku [2C 28]
SIZE 68,800 square metres
RAIL Hatsudai – Keio Line
ACCESS open

Takahiko Yanagisawa / TAK Associated Architects 1997

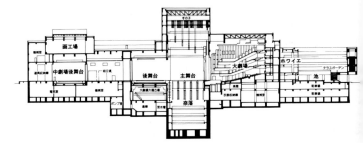

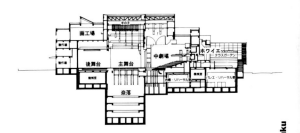

Shinjuku

Takahiko Yanagisawa / TAK Associated Architects 1997

Tokyo Metropolitan Art Space

Ikebukuro is well known for its small alternative theatre companies and 'An-gura' stage arts (a 'Japanglish' word meaning 'underground'). So the Tokyo metropolitan government decided it would be an appropriate site for a massive cultural entertainment complex housing four theatres seating between 2000 and 300 people. The area, near a busy railway station, is made up of small buildings and narrow streets and a 12,440-square-metre site was cleared to make way for the development. The venture was led by bureaucrats and along with some forty art works, the site includes neighbourhood facilities such as a plaza, park and bus stops.

All aspects of this building seem to be derived from commercial department-store design. Exterior walls covering huge volumes are topped with post-modern elements. An emergency exit ramp is hung by rods from projecting triangular plates and at one side of this over-scaled columns frame an entrance. The front façade is dominated by a vast, sloping, triangular glass atrium supported on the inside by a space-frame. A long escalator leads visitors through set of dramaless interior spaces lavishly appointed with gold edging and marble walls. Few of the details are adjusted to a human scale.

ADDRESS 1–8–1 Nishi-ikebukuro, Toshima-ku [4E 34]
STRUCTURAL ENGINEER Takefumi Orimoto Structural Engineer & Associates
CLIENT Tokyo Metropolitan Government
SIZE 49,740 square metres
JR Ikebukuro – Yamanote Line
METRO Ikebukuro – Marunouchi Line
ACCESS open; for more details telephone 03-5391-2111

Shinjuku

Yoshinobu Ashihara 1990

Shinjuku

Yoshinobu Ashihara 1990

North-west Tokyo

Atrium

This apartment block stands out among the many anonymous residential complexes that have been built over the last twenty years. A standardised format has been established by developers with an eye on economy rather than quality of living, producing isolated cells differentiated from each other only by changes in surface materials. As an antidote to such face-lessness, the architects here explored the qualities of 'public and private' represented by the idea of 'figure and ground'. Public spaces such as the inner courtyards and passages at the heart of the project become the main focus or 'figure', while the walls and steps that face on to the courts, treated as planes of vibrant colours, act as backdrops for 'actors'. Hence individual apartments become the 'ground' for the life that goes on on the colourful stage sets.

Geometric architectural elements are set around the open court and passages: a lime and cobalt-blue triangle screens a flight of steps; a black-and-white chequered 'board' positioned diagonally constitutes part of a floor; standing at one corner of this is a golden 'ruined' column by Eiji Yamanoto. In contrast, the outside walls of the block are exposed, sober concrete and the drama springs to life only on crossing the threshold of the double-height porch.

ADDRESS 1–22–1 Shirasagi, Nakano-ku [6C 30]
STRUCTURAL ENGINEER Momota Engineers Inc.
CONTRACTOR Daiei Komuten
SIZE 1000 square metres
RAIL Saginomiya – Seibu Shinjuku Line
ACCESS none

Kunihiko Hayakawa 1985

Kunihiko Hayakawa 1985

Labyrinth

Labyrinth continues the same idea of developing public and private space as Kunihiko Hayakawa's earlier Atrium residential project (see page 240), but it is transfigured with a maze of steps and many interlocking terrace levels. Twenty-two flats in the five-storey building provide homes mainly for young families. All the entrances face the central wide path at the interior of the block and are accessed via steps with white-painted steel handrails. These stand out against wall colours that are more subdued than those of Atrium but nevertheless very chic: pinks and buffs with flashes of turquoise. Although this is less spectacular than the earlier project, the public realm is more open, with a Mediterranean atmosphere conducive to evening strolls and neighbourly chats.

ADDRESS 1–26–8 Igusa, Suginami-ku [1E 32]
STRUCTURAL ENGINEER Gengo Matsui and O.R.S. Office
CONTRACTOR Chiyoda Kensetsu
SIZE 1400 square metres
RAIL Shimo-igusa – Seibu Shinjuku Line
ACCESS public spaces are open

Kunihiko Hayakawa 1989

Kunihiko Hayakawa 1989

Sakuradai Apartment

Coelacanth, a group of young and energetic architects, has seized on the disorder of Tokyo and the changing lifestyles of many of its inhabitants to re-examine the question: 'What is city-dwelling?' The group is interested mainly in the increasing number of young people who flow into Tokyo seeking new opportunities. This five-storey apartment block includes a barber, a restaurant and twelve one-room flats for singles and 'dinkies'.

Until the 1970s, basic wooden apartments were the standard offering. The more affluent city-dwellers of the 1980s demanded more stylish and comfortable living spaces and 'one-room mansions' were built: six or seven tatami mat (180 by 90 cm each)-sized 'bed-sit'-type rooms equipped with mass-produced unit-bathrooms and unit-kitchens, and the obligatory full air conditioning. People live in these anonymous capsule dwellings temporarily, moving out within a few years, and pursuing an existence more or less isolated from traditional group-based society.

Concerned with the idea that the city was becoming an anonymous place to live, Coelacanth responded by endeavouring to assimilate individuals into a larger whole. Thus this one-room mansion should not be seen as part of the city, but as an autonomous whole which itself simulates the arbitrary process by which Tokyo has developed. Each architect within the group contributed a different idea and their designs were collaged together without mediation. Corridors are analogous to twisting streets and rooms to houses. Appropriately, the block is set amid densely packed surrounding buildings of dissimilar materials and types.

The fourth floor was designed as the ground level of the city and the wide terraces are approximately level with the surrounding roof heights. The fifth and sixth floors are set back to avoid blocking light to buildings to the north and the diverse shapes of the rooms form a skyline 'rooftop

Coelacanth Architects 1990

Coelacanth Architects 1990

village'. A skylight is set in the high ceiling of each of the irregularly planned rooms. Kitchens are minimally equipped, with water pipes left exposed. A heavy concrete structural frame, both vertical and angled over, invades the plain rectangular spaces of the lower three 'basement' storeys.

The scheme is let down by the details, which seem too rough and hurried to carry through the ideas.

ADDRESS 2–21–12 Toyotama-kami, Nerima-ku [41 39]
STRUCTURAL ENGINEER T.I.S. & Partners
CLIENT Meisei Company, Ltd
CONTRACTOR Kawabata Kensetsu Company, Ltd
SIZE 700 square metres
RAIL Sakuradai – Seibu Ikebukuro Line
ACCESS none

Coelacanth Architects 1990

North-west Tokyo

Coelacanth Architects 1990

Setagaya

TIT Centennial Anniversary Hall

The Tokyo Institute of Technology is one of Japan's leading academic institutions. The anniversary hall is sited at the northern end of the campus, surrounded by paths and green spaces and next to Ookayama Station. The overhead electric railway cables form a delicate web beside the extraordinary 24-metre-high metallic bulk, which contains exhibition space and conference rooms.

The neighbouring high street of two-storey housing and shops is totally overwhelmed by the new building's composition, if not its size. An aluminium-panelled polygonal form is intersected at its top by a stainless-steel-panelled half-cylinder, 11 metres in diameter and 44 metres long. This is bent at its centre so it emerges from either side of the polygon at different angles. This half-tube, which houses a bar and restaurant, is balanced by complicated forces and seems suspended in mid-air, upsetting the viewer's notions of gravity.

Shinohara's early work used traditional Japanese forms, but during the 1970s he began to explore more abstract ideas of internal space as a monochrome, white 'vessel', divorced from any context, which influenced the early works of Toyo Ito. In the early 1980s, within small housing schemes, his interest moved to composition and the abrupt insertion of brutal structures, a kind of spatial violence. More recently, the relationship of his work to the surrounding city has become the main focus – an issue which is explored in this project.

Shinohara describes the incompatibility that arises when different structures and styles are juxtaposed as 'progressive anarchy'. He explains that when the intensity of the mismatch is extreme, it becomes an 'urban machine' that produces 'random noises' in the viewer's perception. The forms and ideas favoured by the architect are derived from functional designs for extreme environments such as jet fighter planes or the Apollo

Kazuo Shinohara 1987

Kazuo Shinohara 1987

landing capsules.

As in most of Shinohara's work, interior spaces are left plain with exposed concrete or white panels. Services are left fully exposed and some colour is added for contrast. In comparison with its spectacular exterior, the interior of the anniversary hall is dull and warehouse-like – a surpisingly insensitive space given the architect's earlier interests.

ADDRESS 2–12–1 Ookayama, Meguro-ku [31 23]
STRUCTURAL ENGINEER Kimura Structural Engineers and Akira Wada Laboratory
CLIENT Tokyo Institute of Technology
CONTRACTOR joint venture of Taisei, Obayashi, Kajima, Shimizu and Takenaka
CONTRACT VALUE ¥830 million
SIZE 2700 square metres
RAIL Ookayama – Tokyu Mekama Line
ACCESS open 9.30–16.30

Setagaya

Kazuo Shinohara 1987

Setagaya

Kazuo Shinohara 1987

If nothing else, this design studio and car showroom for Mazda proves that Japanese commercial culture can outdo America's Disney, especially during the boom of the 1980s when this building was conceived. Western architectural elements are transformed into pure kitsch; an Ionic column, six storeys high, is farcically overscaled. There is not a glimmer of elegance, intelligence or significance in its demeanour; it is a cultural alien, though certainly striking. Located alongside six lanes of heavy traffic of the Kanpachi-dori, Tokyo's eighth ringroad, the signboard architecture could easily be mistaken for one of the many themed Love Hotels that appear along the highways.

The interior space is surprisingly modern and well articulated. The centre of the column contains a glazed lift with metallic panels which forms the hub of the circulation. The glass-walled section at the south contains offices, while showrooms are set behind a concrete walled area to the north which is cast to look like stone.

ADDRESS 2–4–27 Kinuta, Setagaya-ku [4D 26]
CLIENT Mazda Motor Corporation
CONTRACTOR Kajima Corporation
SIZE 4482 square metres
RAIL Chitosefunabashi – Odakyu Railway
ACCESS open 10.00–19.00

Setagaya

Kengo Kuma & Associates 1991

Kengo Kuma & Associates 1991

Setagaya Art Museum

The Setagaya Art Museum is set in 40 hectares of green parkland ideal for family outings, located in an uptown residential area. When the proposal for the museum was made public, there was concern that the 8000-square-metre building would spoil the existing natural beauty. The issue of 'humanism' became the main tool to persuade people of its appropriateness, and finally the museum was built at the edge of the park, becoming part of a picturesque setting for suburban life.

The architect makes reference to Frank Lloyd Wright's organic architecture. Concrete pergolas are supported by up-ended triangles set on blocks. The interior corridors continue the triangular theme. The building is divided into several pavilions which surround a plaza at basement level. The different volumes all have curved green copper roofs and exterior walls textured by square tiles.

ADDRESS 1–2 Kinuta-koen, Setagaya-ku [5E 26]
STRUCTURAL ENGINEER Gengo Matsui + O.R.S. Office
CLIENT Setagaya Ward
CONTRACTOR joint venture of Shimizu, Muramoto and Maeda
CONTRACT VALUE ¥4 billion
SIZE 8223 square metres
RAIL Yoga – Shin-tamagawa Line
ACCESS open Tuesday to Friday and Sunday, 10.00–18.00; Saturday 10.00–20.00

Setagaya

Shozo Uchii 1985

Koun-ji Temple at Seijo

This Buddhist temple, in an upper-middle-class area of medium-sized houses and gardens, is located in a natural dip 7 metres below street level. Local residents objected to the proposed height and volume of the scheme, with the result that only the traditional sloping black-tiled roof that covers the main hall is visible from the street.

The temple was rebuilt in 1965, but an expansion in activities required further development. The roof levels of most of the new spaces are continuous with the street. A flat roof at the south provides a surface for parking and a flight of steps leads down from street level between the two volumes. The main hall can also be accessed via a bridge from the parking area.

Each aspect of the building is designed to highlight the qualities of a different material. Concrete walls are dissected and glass walls are intersected. The main hall has steel columns in place of the traditional wood and the wooden frames are overlaid. The main architectural ingredients – wood, steel, concrete and glass – are assembled in accordance with what the architect describes as his 'thirty-third experiment in material'.

ADDRESS 7–12–22 Kinuta, Setagaya-ku [5D 26]
STRUCTURAL ENGINEER Yamabe Structural Engineers
CONTRACTOR Takenaka Corporation
SIZE 1870 square metres
RAIL Seijogakuenmae – Odakyu Railway
ACCESS open

Setagaya

Ryoji Suzuki 1991

Setagaya

Ryoji Suzuki 1991

Oda Residence

It is the incompatible juxtaposition of different elements – treated independently so each reads as a discreet piece of sculpture within a powerful installation of details and spaces – that distinguishes the work of Atsushi Kitagawara.

This housing project is divided into two blocks – a long one on the west side and a 5-metre-square one to the east. An independent white steel structure spans the concrete walls and a canvas-covered frame of curved steel beams leaps over the front yard. Projecting into this space from a second-storey yellow cement wall is a 3-metre cube made up of dark blue steel panels. This solid, which seems to rest on a sheet-glass window, contains steps that connect the two volumes.

The eastern block has an 8.5-metre-high void running through its three storeys. Bedrooms lead off at the top level and the living-room in the basement is crossed by a thick black wall which is in fact a cupboard. This space opens through a glazed wall on to a narrow outside area where a grassy slope ascends to ground level.

The result is an assembly of complicated details and potent spaces caught in performance.

ADDRESS 1–20–4 Shimouma, Setagaya-ku [2H 27]
STRUCTURAL ENGINEER Ikeda Structure Design Office
CONTRACTOR Higashiyama Komuten
SIZE 261 square metres
RAIL Yutenji – Tokyu Toyoko Line
ACCESS none

Atsushi Kitagawara 1990

Yoga A-Flat

In a composition reminiscent of Russian Constructivism, two rectangular volumes are placed on either side of a long, narrow (6-metre-wide) inner court with a further rectangle spanning the court at right angles from their roofs. This complex consists of eight maisonettes with a small hall for shared activities. Each split-level dwelling is 4.5 metres high with low 2.1-metre ceilings on each floor and its own open space.

All aspects of the dwellings are minimal. The walls are plain, coloured light grey, and the steel-tube stairs that cross each room to the higher level are lightweight and simple. The kitchens are designed as moveable units made up of an electric cooker, stainless-steel worktop and sink on casters. One of the bathrooms is also designed by the architect, fully exposed by a transparent poly-carbonate wall. A freestanding frame has a sink and toilet on opposite sides, topped by a moveable shaving mirror.

The stylish atmosphere is aimed at design-related professionals. In contrast to the architect's earlier housing schemes, Atrium and Labyrinth (see pages 240 and 242), this project caters for Tokyo dwellers with more private home-lives rather than seeking to encourage an interactive community.

ADDRESS 3–1–17 Kami-yoga, Setagaya-ku [5F 27]
STRUCTURAL ENGINEER Momota Engineers Inc.
CONTRACTOR Kadowaki Kensetsu
SIZE 685 square metres
RAIL Yoga – Shin-tamagawa Line
ACCESS none

Kunihiko Hayakawa 1993

Kunihiko Hayakawa 1993

South Tokyo
(Yokohama)

Yokohama Museum of Art

Yokohama developed as a major port, but shipping has moved south and the docks and wharves now lie idle. Many of the 3 million inhabitants commute into Tokyo to work, reducing Yokohama to a suburb or satellite town. In order to regenerate the city, a total of 186 hectares of the dock area has been renamed Minatomirai (Future Port), with the aim of providing employment for 190,000 office workers by the 21st century. The Yokohama Museum of Art is located at the centre of this area. Tange took the opportunity to include an axial approach road from the front of the building to the bayside, with a public vista point at the top of a tower looking out over the development-to-be. This semicircular tower, 45 metres high, is situated in the middle of an 180-metre-long three-storey building. The exterior is entirely panelled in pale grey Italian granite and pale pink Spanish granite. Classical proportions and a symmetrical layout reinforce the central axis. A 100-metre-long 'grand gallery', also uniformly panelled in pastel granites, runs from the entrance.

(See *Godzilla vs Mosra*, in which Tokyo's favourite monster lays to waste the entire development area in yet another epic battle set among architectural landmarks.)

ADDRESS 3–4 Minatomirai, Nishi-ku Yokohama-shi, Kanagawa Prefecture [1F 97]
STRUCTURAL ENGINEER Takumi Orimoto & Associates
CONTRACTOR joint venture of Takenaka, Shimizu, Okumura, Tokyu, Sato and Nara
SIZE 26,830 square metres
JR Sakuragicho – Negishi Line
RAIL Sakuragicho – Tokyu Toyoko Line
ACCESS open Friday to Wednesday, 10.00–18.00

Kenzo Tange Associates 1989

South Tokyo (Yokohama)

Kenzo Tange Associates 1989

Shukoh Office Building

This office building and factory is located 15 kilometres south of central Tokyo, near the heavy-industrial area of Kawasaki. The building has an unusual façade and uses a wide range of mass-produced materials. Though these are nominally functional and go largely unnoticed in such an area, the imaginative way the architect has employed them transforms them from the prosaic to the poetic.

The building is divided into two totally different parts. The larger section, set at the back, includes a factory floor, warehouse and two office floors. A frame of undulating steel pipes supports a striking roof of wired corrugated glass. Three large jointed parasols shade the double-height office spaces below.

The other section, containing an entrance hall, showroom, reception room and executive suite, faces the street. Vertical fins made of glass-reinforced-concrete panels project from the concave façade walls. A circular staircase at the corner of the building is set behind 'folded' mirror glass and curved walls made of perforated corrugated-steel panels, topped by a shallow domed roof. The juxtaposition of so many different materials and forms creates a rich and dynamic architecture.

ADDRESS 2–2–10 Yaguchi, Ota-ku [4C 24]
STRUCTURAL ENGINEER Nippon Steel Corporation and Skeleton A.D.O. Company, Ltd
CONTRACTOR Taisei Corporation
SIZE 3634 square metres
RAIL Musashi-nitta – Tokyu Mekama Line
ACCESS none

South Tokyo (Yokohama)

TAO Architects 1989

TAO Architects 1989

Yamato International

As you drive east along Kan-nana-dori (Tokyo's seventh ringroad) towards Tokyo Bay, a collection of gleaming roofs appears, floating like a summer cloud behind the treetops of a park.

This is the headquarters of a fashion company – a narrow building, 23 by 130 metres, with nine storeys. The lower three constitute a 'base' hidden behind the treeline, the highest approximately level with the traffic that flows over the nearby elevated bridge. This base contains warehouse space, and large distribution bays open from it on to a parking area that occupies half the site to the east. This eastern frontage is relatively plain with few windows. The western façade, which overlooks the park, is more elaborate, its multiple terraces and wide picture windows taking full advantage of the view.

The inspiration for the distinctive design was the architect's studies of vernacular Mediterranean villages, their complex appearance arising from their different roofs and varied architectural elements. 'Multiple scenes' was the key term used to create Hara's communicative design.

The exterior is a composition of figurative features, in particular the curved, cumulus-shaped roofs, together with others that are inclined, pitched and sometimes glazed. These are dramatically layered, and narrow, square and triangular windows and gridded frames form discontinuous patterns among them. The shadows cast by the layered forms, the reflection of the sky within the many windows and the employment of a single material – aluminium – help to mould the complex into a cohesive whole.

The interior space is less successful. Many design components continue the themes of the facade. Figures such as clouds, grids and triangles are used as graphic elements and layered to produce screens for lighting, walls, ceilings, windows and doors. These patterns also reflect the archi-

Hiroshi Hara 1986

Hiroshi Hara 1986

tect's interest in mathematical theory. Otherwise, the spaces are left plain and the offices are a far cry from the rich spatial sequences of the villages to which the scheme refers.

At twilight, the scene is dramatically transformed: the aluminium panels reflect the reds of the sunset and deep black shadows from the roofs are inscribed on the façade. As night falls, the effect, changing second-by-second, is breathtaking.

South Tokyo (Yokohama)

ADDRESS 5–1–1 Heiwajima, Ota-ku [3G 25]
STRUCTURAL ENGINEER Sano Structural Engineers
CONTRACTOR joint venture of Obayashi, Shimizu and Nomura
SIZE 12,000 square metres
RAIL Heiwajima – Keihin Kyuko Line
ACCESS none

Hiroshi Hara 1986

Hiroshi Hara 1986

Tower of Winds

In the Tower of Winds, Toyo Ito represents the visual complexity of Tokyo metaphorically in terms of a never-ceasing, ever-changing wind. In contrast to the west, where the city is perceived as a permanent museum of monuments and spaces, Ito sees Tokyo as ephemeral, articulated not through its buildings, but through electricity pylons and vending machines, illuminated advertisements and traffic signals; it is the small scale, the temporary and the chance encounter that define his city. Light fulfils both a physical and metaphoric role: the city undergoes a complete transformation when after sundown its fictional state is revealed – 'although buildings proclaim their existence in the daytime, they lose their sense of reality at night'.

The Tower of Winds represents the city through a constantly moving spectacle of light. A 21-metre-high oval cylinder stands at the centre of a roundabout, constantly clogged with buses and taxis, just in front of the busy JR Yokohama Station. During the day it is a grey part of the scenery of department stores, banks and office buildings. But as the sun goes down, it becomes a sensual device both describing and recording the transitory state of the city.

Perforated aluminium panels are supported on a lightweight structure which conceals a ventilation tower for a vast underground shopping mall, transforming a mundane chimney into an elegant column. Acrylic mirrors are placed on the ventilation tower; between these and the aluminium panels are set more than 1000 mini-lamps and twelve neon rings. Thirty floodlights are set at the base. The lights are computer-programmed to produce changing patterns derived from information collected from the environment.

At dusk a symphony of light transforms the tower into a shimmering spectacle of dancing lights and shifting transparency. Neon lights travel

Toyo Ito 1986

up and down the height of the cylinder and the surface of the panels appears and disappears, alternately solid and diaphanous as the flood-lights change in response to the wind direction and spped. The myriad of mini-lamps, which react to the surrounding noise, create patterns of stardust.

With its prosaic daytime presence, reference to temporary structures and spectral nocturnal life, the Tower of Winds presents the city of Toyo Ito's imagination.

ADDRESS Kita-saiwai, Nishi-ku Yokohama-shi, Kanagawa Prefecture [3C 96]
STRUCTURAL ENGINEER Gengo Matsui and O.R.S. Office
LIGHT DESIGN TL Yamagiwa Laboratory
CLIENT Yokohama Station Promotional Committee
CONTRACTOR Obayashi Corporation
JR Yokohama – Tokaido Line
RAIL Yokohama – Tokyu Toyoko Line
ACCESS open

Toyo Ito 1986

Toyo Ito 1986

Sotetsu Bunka Kaikan

A cultural core containing a gallery, seminar rooms and studios stands among newly built high-rise residential buildings. The architect describes the building as a 'receiver' of ethereal information, though in fact it is the viewer who invests the architecture with this characteristic.

Six 'wings' are placed on the roof as symbolic receptors, like aerials picking up messages in the airwaves. These are supported by galvanised-steel truss frames. Concrete columns below the wings line the approach steps to the gallery spaces on the fourth floor.

South Tokyo (Yokohama)

ADDRESS 4–3–28 Ryokuen, Izumi-ku Yokohama-shi, Kanagawa Prefecture [3H 109]
STRUCTURAL ENGINEER Sano Structural Engineers
CLIENT Sagami Railway (Sotetsu)
CONTRACTOR Sotetsu Construction
SIZE 3870 square metres
RAIL Ryokuentoshi – Sagami Railway
ACCESS gallery is open

Hiroshi Hara 1990

South Tokyo (Yokohama)

Hiroshi Hara 1990

Housing in Ryokuentoshi

Ryokuentoshi, which literally translated means 'green-garden-city', is one of the new towns conceived and developed by Japan's railway companies. A new railway line is laid across the countryside and huge amounts of money are invested in housing schemes and commercial facilities based around a station. Much of the natural landscape around greater Tokyo has already disappeared under schemes by Keio, Odakyu and Seibu Railways. This area, Ryokuentoshi, is now being developed by Sagami Railway (Sotetsu).

The new town has been in progress since the 1980s and is not yet completed. Streets have been laid out, but many sites have yet to be filled by the prefabricated houses of suburban dreams. Riken Yamamoto was invited to design the buildings in the town centre, though he was not involved in the urban planning, so the buildings were designed individually. But a sense of continuity is maintained by the use of the same materials throughout and the passages that connect some of the buildings. These were designed singly and each picks up on the former dewsign to produce a sequential consistency with rich and various differences.

Seven buildings have been completed and an eighth is under construction. There are shops on the first and second floors and flats on the top two storeys. The reinforced-concrete structures are clad with concrete 'bricks' and have wide windows.

Galvanised-steel frames support terraces, bridges and walkways, providing what is in effect another ground level, a city in the air. These public spaces are protected from the elements by lightweight roofs suspended from thin steel columns and numerous tension rods. The impression of work-in-progress lent by the 'scaffolding' perhaps owes something to the unpredictable development of traditional Asian villages, translated into neat modern materials.

Riken Yamamoto and Field Shop 1992–93

South Tokyo (Yokohama)

XYSTUS, 2686 square metres, April 1992

G F Building, 807 square metres, November 1992

ARCUS, 2978 square metres, February 1993

OBERISK, 2518 square metres, March 1993

LOGGIA, 887 square metres, April 1993

AMNIS, 1332 square metres, July 1993

PRADO, 1481 square metres, December 1993

ADDRESS Ryokuentoshi, Izumi-ku, Yokohama-shi, Kanagawa
Prefecture [3H 109]
STRUCTURAL ENGINEER Imai Consulting Structural Engineer, Kozo
Keikaku Plus One, Dan Engineering, Creative Design Research
CLIENT Sagami Railway
CONTRACTOR Sotetsu Construction, Nishimatsu Construction
RAIL Ryokuentoshi – Sagami Railway
ACCESS open

South Tokyo (Yokohama)

Riken Yamamoto and Field Shop 1992–93

Shonandai Culture Centre

The urban hinterland of metropolitan Tokyo gives way to anonymous buildings strung along the roadside which gradually coalesce into a denser, though incoherent development interspersed with parking lots. This project provides a much-needed communal heart, as well as a space for cultural activities and recreation.

Alone among the finalists in the 1986 competition, Itsuko Hasegawa rejected an historicist, formulaic approach, avoiding banal quotations from the repertory of world architecture: the Mayan temple, the agora, the amphitheatre. With a playful sense of decoration, she has assembled shells, marbles, fragments of coloured glass and animal footprints among fairytale silver 'trees', a river and two cosmic spheres. The scheme provides an enthralling setting for a performance billed as 'second nature' in an architecture Hasegawa describes as an 'artificial landscape'.

Two large metallic spheres dominate the site. The larger, 37-metre-diameter 'cosmic globe' houses the civic theatre. The smaller 'terrestial globe', set higher and covered in aluminium panels on which is etched a map of the world, contains a planetarium. These stand amid many pointed roofs of buildings and small shelters, their points and facets reminiscent of crystal growths. The exterior walls of the site are ochre-coloured concrete. Geological layers or 'strata' are traced over these on the streetside, giving the impression of geological faults thrown up by the earth's movement.

The main approach is via undulating stainless-steel pergolas hung with vines and squares of stained glass that cast dappled colours on to the paving. Finally the full extent of this wonderous land – some 30 metres wide and 80 metres long – is revealed. Immediately to the right, on a platform above a pond sparkling with mosaics of coloured glass, is the 'tree of light and wind'. Delicate perforated aluminium strips, frozen in a wind-

Itsuko Hasegawa 1990

Itsuko Hasegawa 1990

swept movement, wind around a structure of thin columns. A metal weathercock flies from the crown. Against the light, an inner chrome frame is visible through the 'leaves'.

Further metal trees grow in this garden, one of which is an elaborate mechanical clock that marks the hours with whirring noises and flashing lights. Beyond, the terrestrial globe can be seen suspended above the ground, resting on buildings at either side. Directly below its South Pole a spring bubbles up into a small pond surrounded by dark bricks – the source of a river that flows through the centre of the land.

The entrance to the children's museum and planetarium is set below the globe and to the right. Behind stepped glass walls lurk gigantic models of insects and animals. The civic centre is entered on the left, where a curved wall of glass blocks leads to a spacious double-height lobby. Seventy per cent of the space is underground, including a gymnasium, meeting rooms, kitchens and so on. Each space is bright and cheerful and looks out through glazed walls on to sunken gardens with earthen walls, as if cut from the earth's strata.

Passing under the globe is the entrance to the civic theatre. A steel geodesic dome is infilled with thick concrete panels sprayed with aluminium,which shut out noise. A calm, larger-scaled open area is crossed by a high-level bridge leading to the ochre walls that border the site – part of a circular route that begins with a path beside the pond from which curved steps lead up to the top of the walls and wind above the museum, where one follows the pattern of animal footprints imprinted in the tiles.

This overtly sentimental 'cast' has been compared to the thematic exposition pavilions that arose during the 1980s, in which the accepted terms of architecture and 'gravitas' are clearly bypassed. However, any

Itsuko Hasegawa 1990

South Tokyo (Yokohama)

Itsuko Hasegawa 1990

misgivings about this fantasy affair will be dispelled by a visit. Despite its extraordinary appearance in the centre of a very ordinary town, the scheme's success can be clearly measured by its popularity – by midday children are running riot over every square inch of the project, while parents retire to sit at shaded café tables. Corridors and rooms are filled with local people using the facilities, attending classes or meeting friends. It only remains to join them – to explore and be swept up in Hasegawa's magical landscape.

South Tokyo (Yokohama)

ADDRESS 1–8 Shonandai, Fujisawa-shi, Kanagawa Prefecture [4G 109]
STRUCTURAL ENGINEER Kimura Structural Engineers, Umezawa Design Office
CLIENT Fujisawa City
CONTRACTOR Obayashi Corporation
CONTRACT VALUE ¥4 billion
SIZE 14,315 square metres
RAIL Shonandai – Odakyu Enoshima Line
ACCESS Tuesday to Sunday, 9.00–17.00

Itsuko Hasegawa 1990

South Tokyo (Yokohama)

West Tokyo

Truss Wall House

Ushida-Findlay is a dual-nationality architectural practice whose work has evolved from a synthesis of the cultural backgrounds of the partners: Japan and Britain. While other Japanese architects tend to pursue more or less similar issues, the studio manages to introduce provocative and stimulating themes into their work.

This project, a home for a young family, is situated in a commuter 'bed town' an hour and a half from Tokyo. Immediately beside the Odakyu railwayline stands a strongly tactile and emotive white sculptural form – or, more aptly, an 'organ'. Various taut and freeform curves are made in reinforced concrete by means of the client's patented 'truss wall' construction method and the application of computer-aided design. The small space – two storeys on a 100-square-metre site – is maximised in relation to both the thermal environment and the topological flow of bodily movement.

The schematically hollowed-out interior is enclosed by a double-wall envelope, with insulation and air cavities between, so the walls become a second skin functioning as a 'thermo-dynamic organ' that stabilises the environment inside. The circulation corresponds to bodily movement through the spaces that are intentionally interconnected like a Möbius band. The architects 'intended to create space, as a fluid continuity of sensuousness and physical imagery which is disseminated with a person's movement through that space.' The volumes 'emulate the flow of pliable viscera which is packed into a vessel' and become a 'frozen fluidity'.

A living and dining area on the upper floor is reached by six steps up from the street. On entering, one follows the flow of walls with 'soft', hand-brushed mortar surfaces; stairs lead down to bedrooms on the lower floor and a long wall leads to a kitchen with built-in shelves at the far end of the room. A round seating area has a built-in sofa under a, 'egg'

Ushida Findlay Partnership 1993

Ushida Findlay Partnership 1993

dome-shaped ceiling. Glass doors open on to a tiny courtyard floored with tiles made from coloured mortar cast in balloons; an opening that absorbs both heat and light into the interior. A flight of steps ascends to a small rooftop garden, and a distinctive handrail forms the rail.

ADDRESS Machida-shi [4H 75]
STRUCTURAL ENGINEER Tanaka Studio at Waseda University
CONTRACTOR Truss Wall
SIZE 70 square metres
RAIL Tsurukawa – Odakyu Odawara Line
ACCESS none

West Tokyo

Ushida Findlay Partnership 1993

Ushida Findlay Partnership 1993

Fog-Forest Park

The Fog-Forest Park is located at the north-west end of the extensive Showa Memorial Park – a popular setting for a day out that includes cherry blossom trees, a 'bouncy mountain', and a lido. But the Fog-Forest Park adds a different dimension – a powerful and elemental zone in which the insubstantiality of mist and tangibility of architecture are interwoven. Fujiko Nakaya, the sculptress of mist, invited Atsushi Kitagawara to design the landscape and features for the project, and the scheme represents a collaboration of two distinctive designers.

The site is a grid of small grassy hillocks with a network of paths between. Near the centre lies a wide, square basin. Its concrete sides slope down to a central square vent and further vents are set around its upper edges. From these emanate slow curls of mist and hissing sounds. The basin fills and the 'heavier-than-air' cold fog spills out, crawling between the mounds to engulf their stark geometry in its enigmatic drapery.

The children who rush to watch the process at first stand wary and hesitant, but are soon irresistibly drawn to plunge through the paths into the cool swirls. At this point a long cylinder of perforated aluminium panels, carelessly balanced on a slope at the edge of the site, comes into play. Mist seeps out of its pores, building up to a billowing mass that then sinks down among the mounds, paths and delighted faces.

ADDRESS Showa Memorial Park, Tachikawa-shi [4G 59]
STRUCTURAL ENGINEER Nelsa-Cobo
CONTRACTOR Nelsa-Cobo, Kubota
SIZE 430 square metres
JR Tachikawa – Chuo Line
ACCESS 9.30–17.00 (perfomances: 12.00–15.00 on weekdays and 10.00–16.00 on weekends, every 30 minutes)

West Tokyo

Atsushi Kitagawara + ILCD 1992

Atsushi Kitagawara + ILCD 1992

Amusement Complex

Tama New Town, located in Tokyo's 'bed town' belt, has developed over the last twenty years. At its heart, Tama Centre, is a vast new commercial area including a 'Parthenon' and other garish theme-park buildings. But the area surrounding the city's second main station, Nagayama, was featureless and unfashionable until Toyo Ito's floating 'UFOs' provided a focus. A small irregular polygon stands above a pedestrian deck and a further building is a vast elliptical volume panelled with aluminium seems to float above a glass-walled space.

The floating effect of the ellipse is achieved through its continuous curved base, visually uninterrupted by supporting walls, which rests on a series of elegant white columns and glass. The entrance is on the third-floor level, and the fourth floor is designed as an 'open-air rooftop' containing the curved indoor roofs over many of the other areas, while the sky is represented by the underbelly curve of the ellipse. The decor is cool and sophisticated with metallic elements.

A large proportion of the space is occupied by 'Healthy Land', a company that offers baths, saunas and party and relaxation rooms to local people, especially the older generation. Colourful plastic flowers and wholly inappropriate signs and advertisements welcoming customers invade Ito's refined space.

ADDRESS 1–3–4 Nagayama, Tama-shi [4F 71]
STRUCTURAL ENGINEER Gengo Matsui and O.R.S. Office
CLIENT Humax Estate
CONTRACTOR joint venture of Kumagai and Nishimatsu
SIZE 4570 square metres
RAIL Nagayama – Keio Line, Odakyu Railway
ACCESS open

West Tokyo

Toyo Ito 1992

Toyo Ito 1992

Tokyo Salesian Boys' Home

A small Catholic school (established for orphans after the war) deliberately eschews the hedonism of the 1980s. Instead, the design draws on purist and Modernist themes, with a plain but powerful composition of materials: exposed concrete, wooden floors and wooden furniture. Long, sloping roofs with earthen-coloured tiles cover ten schoolhouses and dormitories arranged around a central green reminiscent of an English village. A chapel with an irregular polygon plan is located at the eastern end alongside a high belltower.

The interior of the chapel is lit by windows on either side of the altar and openings at the top of the walls from which light falls behind twelve multi-faceted columns. The ceiling, a triangular network of massive concrete beams, is 8 metres high and appears to float above a wall that stretches behind the altar. A cross is cut out of the centre of this wall through which light falls on to the aisle. A peaceful calm pervades the space, and the sacredness of religion is well represented.

ADDRESS 4–7–1 Josui-minami-cho,
Kodaira-shi [5G 78]
STRUCTURAL ENGINEER Kozo Keikaku
Engineering
CONTRACTOR Toda Construction,
Japan Development Construction
SIZE 7530 square metres
JR Kokubunji – Chuo Line
ACCESS ask for permission at reception

West Tokyo

Sakakura Associates Architects and Engineers 1990

Index

Tokyo: a guide to recent architecture

Tokyo: a guide to recent architecture

Tokyo: a guide to recent architecture

Tokyo: a guide to recent architecture

Tokyo: a guide to recent architecture

Other architecture guides

London A GUIDE TO RECENT ARCHITECTURE
Samanthan Hardingham
Despite the tackiness of many of the buildings spawned during the 1980s' financial boom and the contraction of opportunity resulting from the subsequent recession, a lot of good architecture has been built in London during the last decade. This book, a 1994 AIA award winner, describes one hundred projects from this period, covering all the best, and a few of the worst.

Chicago A GUIDE TO RECENT ARCHITECTURE
Susanna Sirefman
The 'home of the skyscraper', inheritor of the legacy of Frank Lloyd Wright and the Prairie School, and one of the most important sites of Mies van der Rohe's pioneering Modernism, Chicago has been at the forefront of architecture for the last century. This book chronicles the current architecture scene, covering the work of established firms and the new stars.

Los Angeles A GUIDE TO RECENT ARCHITECTURE
Dian Phillips-Pulverman
The current image of Los Angeles architecture has been largely shaped by books, magazines and exhibitions that focus on the work of the 'LA School', represented most famously by architects such as Frank Gehry, and Morphosis, and by that of a younger generation that includes Michele Saee, O'Herlihy + Warner and studio bau:ton.

⋮

Prague A GUIDE TO TWENTIETH-CENTURY ARCHITECTURE
Ivan Margolius
Prague is an overwhelming city: buildings from many periods are arranged like theatrical scenery, modern, hard-edged structures mingle with soft Baroque or Secessionist façades, towers and spires are silhouetted against a backdrop of wavy, red-tiled roofs. This book explores twentieth–century Prague, selecting some 120 buildings from perhaps 1500 of architectural interest.

England A GUIDE TO RECENT ARCHITECTURE
Samantha Hardingham
Pockets of outstandingly successful contemporary architecture are to be found throughout England, often swamped by acres of indifferent or bad building. This new guide identifies the concentrations of the good and presents a survey of the range of current architecture, highlighting the diversity and quality of recent work.

Availability subject to change without notice.   **⋮**

Picture credits